From Alexandrovsk to Zyrardow

A GUIDE TO YIVO'S LANDSMANSHAFTN ARCHIVE

By Rosaline Schwartz
and Susan Milamed

ייִדישער װיסנשאַפֿטלעכער אינסטיטוט — ייִװאָ
YIVO INSTITUTE FOR JEWISH RESEARCH
New York, 1986

Cover photo: Fifteenth anniversary banquet, Progressive Samborer Young Men's Benevolent Association, New York, 1925. (Donated by the Progressive Samborer Young Men's Benevolent Association)

Illustration on frontispiece from a hand water-coloured card from the hospital committee in Radzivilov congratulating the society in New York on its 20th anniversary. (Donated by the Radziviller-Woliner Benevolent Association)

Copyright © 1986 by YIVO Institute for Jewish Research

All rights reserved. No part of this work covered by the copyrights hereon may be reproduced or used in any form or by any means—graphic, electronic, or mechanical, including photocopying, recording, taping, or information storage and retrieval systems—without the prior written permission of the publisher.

ISBN 0-914512-42-0

Library of Congress Catalog Card Number 85-052411

TABLE OF CONTENTS

Acknowledgments i

Landsmanshaftn and Individual Contributors
to the Publication of
"A Guide to YIVO's Landsmanshaftn Archive" iii

Introduction v

Landsmanshaftn Archive: Scope and Content vii

Organization of the Guide ix

Section A: Locality-Based Society Records 1

Section B: Non-Locality Based Society Records 67

Appendix I: Materials received after completion of
              the Landsmanshaftn Project 75

Appendix II: Subject Collection: Landsmanshaftn 76

Appendix III: Locations of Jewish Cemeteries in
              New York City and Environs 85

Index 87

Map: The Second Polish Republic, 1921-1939 .... Insert

Mr. Jacob Finkelstein, secretary of the United Brisker Relief, presents his society's records to Rosaline Schwartz, Landsmanshaftn Project Director (at right) and Susan Milamed, Project Assistant (at left), YIVO Institute, July 17, 1980. Born in Brisk in 1891, Mr. Finkelstein served as Relief secretary for 64 years. He died in November, 1983.

Quotation from letter written by Mr. Finkelstein to accompany his donation:

It is hard to part with you, my dear papers. For 65 years you lay upon my shelves. I protected you and always took you with me when I moved to another apartment...

Who more than you can bear witness to so many experiences: the loss of six million, two world wars, revolutions, a pogrom in Brisk in 1937. So much work accomplished, so much help given in 65 years. So many good people...

It is nearly a year that I have been sitting with you, my dear papers—hundreds of faces, thousands of names pass before me. They were such good people, devoted to the work, with so much patriotism for the Relief up until the end of their lives. They are all gone, but in these papers, their names will remain forever. It is so hard to part with you, my historic papers.

    J. Finkelstein,
    Executive secretary

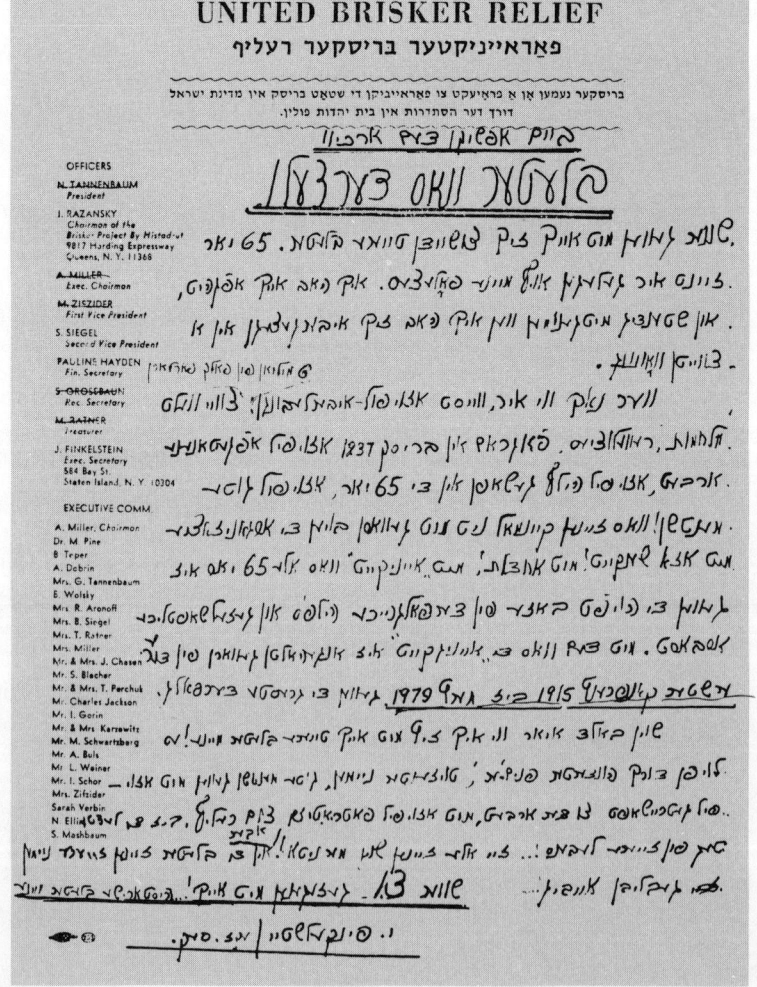

ACKNOWLEDGMENTS

The YIVO Institute is deeply grateful to the National Historical Publications and Records Commission of the National Archives (NHPRC) for funding the *Landsmanshaftn* Project which made possible the establishment of the *Landsmanshaftn* Archive and the preparation of this guide. The encouragement of Frank G. Burke, Acting Archivist of the United States (formerly NHPRC Executive Director), throughout the duration of the project contributed immeasurably to its successful completion. Above all, we are grateful to the hundreds of societies which donated their records to the *Landsmanshaftn* Archive. It is thanks to them that the over 100 year history of *landsmanshaftn* in the United States will be preserved at the YIVO Institute.

On behalf of the YIVO Institute for Jewish Research, I express appreciation to the many institutions that assisted us in locating New York *landsmanshaftn* and their records: Jechil Dobekirer, Joseph Masliansky, and the late Norman Gilmovsky, of the Council of Organizations of the United Jewish Appeal; the late Raymond Gebiner, Council of Organizations of HIAS; Michael Michalovic, formerly of United Organizations for Israel, Histadrut; Israel Figa, Workmen's Circle; Arie Frankel, formerly of Bnai Zion; Leonard Minches, formerly Special Deputy Superintendent in Charge, State of New York Insurance Department Liquidation Bureau, and Anthony Palazollo, Supervisor, Fund Liquidation Department. To the many funeral parlor directors, hotel managers, community center directors, and cemetery supervisors who provided initial contacts with the societies, thanks are given. A special note of appreciation is expressed for the cooperation given by the late Director of Chelsea Hall, Dave Miara, who provided access to this important *landsmanshaftn* meeting hall and shared his deep knowledge of the societies.

I wish to thank all the volunteers who gave so generously of their time in collecting *landsmanshaftn* records, publicizing the project, and preparing voluminous mailings: Rosemary Leighton, Jacob

Lipner, Olive Lieberman, Pauline Finkelstein, the late Elizabeth Field, and intern Carol King. I am deeply appreciative of project assistant Susan Milamed's dedicated efforts on behalf of the project and her wholehearted participation in preparing the guide. The excellent contributions made in collecting and organizing the *landsmanshaftn* materials made by project staff members Esther Blickstein, Lila Everett and Eli Lederhendler are reflected in the scope and organization of the *Landsmanshaftn* Archive.

My special thanks to Samuel Norich, Executive Director of the YIVO Institute for his constant support and encouragement in publishing the guide. I am indebted to the entire YIVO staff for their invaluable support, particularly Marek Web, Head Archivist; Dina Abramowicz, Chief Librarian; Zachary Baker, Associate Librarian during the project; and Lucjan Dobroszycki, Research Associate. I am grateful to Annette Harchik for her expert technical assistance. It was a pleasure to consult with Dr. Arthur A. Goren who by providing historical perspective helped define goals. Most especially I want to thank Dr. Barbara Kirshenblatt-Gimblett for guiding the grant application and for her deep interest over the course of the project.

Rosaline Schwartz
Landsmanshaftn Project Director
YIVO Institute for Jewish Research
January 1986

LANDSMANSHAFTN AND INDIVIDUAL CONTRIBUTORS TO THE PUBLICATION OF "A GUIDE TO YIVO'S LANDSMANSHAFTN ARCHIVE"

A special thanks from the YIVO Institute to Mr. Osias Biller for his generous contribution.

Patrons

Landsmanshaftn
Radomysler Benevolent Society, Inc.

Sponsors

Landsmanshaftn
Boyerker Benevolent Society/Boyerker Heimishe Yugent/Boyerker Emergency Fund

Donors

Landsmanshaftn
Bessarabian Young Men's Benevolent and Educational Club
B'nai Eleazar, Inc.
Chmielniker Sick and Benevolent Society of Poland, Inc.
Czenstochauer Young Men, Inc.
Independent American Lasker Association, Inc.
Independent Meseritzer Young Men's Society
Kudryncer Benevolent Society, Inc.
Lodzer Young Men's Benevolent Society
New Cracow Friendship Society

Individuals
Morris Awerbuch (Husiatyner-Podolier Friendship Circle)
Leo J. Feld

Friends

Landsmanshaftn
Bessarabier Podolier Benevolent Society, Inc.
Bogopoler Unterstutzungs Verein
Chevra Ahavath Abraham B'nai Kolo
Chevra Bnei Israel Anshei Zurow
Congregation Anshei Krashnik
First Beitcher Sick and Benevolent Society

First Nadworna Sick and Benevolent Association
First Zdunska Wola Benevolent Society
Gluboker Benevolent Society
Husiatyner-Podolier Friendship Circle
Husiatyner-Podolier Friendship Circle, Cemetery Fund
Independent Drobniner Benevolent Association
Independent Skierniewicer Benevolent Association, Inc.
Kartuz-Berezer Benevolent Association, Inc.
Kletzker Young Men's Benevolent Association
Ludwig-Field-Altschuler Family Circle
Lukower and Mezricher Society of Los Angeles
New Drohobyczer and Boryslawer Benevolent Association
Piotrkov Trybunalski Relief Association, Inc.
Poloner Independent Aid Society, Inc.
Progressive Samborer Young Men's Benevolent Association
Rohatyner Young Men's Society, Inc.
Shepetovker Young Men's Association
Skalar Benevolent Society
Stanislauer Progressive Benevolent Association
Tarnobrzeg Dzikow Young Men's Association
Trembowla Brotherhood Benevolent Society, Inc.
United Kolbuszower Relief Association
United Pruziner and Vicinity Relief Association
Verchiver Benevolent Society

Individuals
Ruth Eisenstein (Keidaner Association)
Norman Furman (Ratchever-Volyner Aid Association)
Gertrude Greenberg (Husiatyner-Podolier Friendship Circle, Inc.)
Edward Kandel (First Zguritzer-Bessarabier Society)
Martha Rogos (United Ostrower Relief Committee, Ostrow-Mazowieck)
Mr. and Mrs. Nathan Solomon and Family (Progressive Samborer Young Mens' Benevolent Association)

Contributors

Landsmanshaftn
Buczaczer American Benevolent Society
Dobryner Young Folks, Inc.
Dzalishitzer Benevolent Association, Inc.
Fraternal Order of Bendin-Sosnowicer
Grodner-Lipkaner Branch #74, Workmen's Circle
Jacob Sheinbach Family Circle
Kolomear Friends Association
Meshbisher Untershtitsungs Verein
Moses Family Society, Inc.
Sandzer Society, Inc.
Sokolover Young Friends Progressive Aid Society
United Meseritzer Relief, Inc.
Wieloner Benevolent Association
Wisoko-Litowsker B.U.V.

Individuals
Martin Choina (Sokolover Young Friends Progressive Aid Society)
Charles Feder (Fraternal Order of Bendin-Sosnowicer)

 INTRODUCTION

The YIVO Institute for Jewish Research (*Yidisher visnshaftlekher institut*—YIVO) was founded in Vilna, Poland, in 1925. Its headquarters was relocated to New York in 1940. YIVO serves as a teaching, research, and resource center in the areas of East and Central European Jewish history; the Holocaust; Jewish mass immigration and settlement in the United States; and in Yiddish language, literature, folklore, and ethnography.

Central to the Institute's activities are its library and archives. YIVO's multilingual library houses over 300,000 volumes, including the world's largest collection of Yiddish books, and rare volumes of Judaica dating from the 16th century. The archives is a major resource for the study of all aspects of East European Jewish life in Europe and the areas to which Jews migrated. The archives is organized into over 1,200 record groups consisting of 9,000 linear feet of materials, much of which was dramatically rescued after World War II.

In 1979, the National Historical Publications and Records Commission (NHPRC), an affiliate of the National Archives, awarded a grant to the YIVO Institute to fund the *Landsmanshaftn* Project—a two-year effort to salvage the records of *landsmanshaftn*, Jewish mutual-aid societies formed by immigrants originating from the same villages, towns, and cities in Eastern Europe. *Landsmanshaftn* were most prolific in New York where they numbered 6,000 at their peak in the early 1950's. In existence for over 100 years, *landsmanshaftn* were a spontaneous organizational movement growing out of the pressing, common needs of immigrants. At first, the newly-arrived "chipped in" to provide aid for a sick friend; funds for burial; a place to worship; money to bring a *landsman* (countryman) to the United States. Soon, however, these functions were formalized as *landsmanshaftn* began to evolve along democratic lines based on both their members' experience with the communal structure of their Euopean communities and procedures of lodges and fraternal orders which they encountered in America. Led by a highly motivated, non-elitist immigrant leadership, societies incorporated themselves; printed constitutions with rules of order; decided on burial procedures; and arranged for endowments and interest-free loans. While easing their members' adjustment to life in America, societies set up emergency committees or separate relief organizations to send aid to their home towns.

Landsmanshaftn, though, had not only an economic function but were social as well. Many societies began as literary or culture clubs, with activities expressing their members' youthful zest and absorption of American ways as well as their experience with the old world communal (*kehillah*) structure and contemporary political and social movements. The scholarly disregard, however, of the *landsmanshaftn* movement together with the *landsmanshaftn's* own underestimation of the historical value of their records resulted in the almost total loss of *landsmanshaftn* records. As a result of the timely award of the NHPRC grant, the YIVO Institute now houses the *Landsmanshaftn* Archive, the only substantial collection of materials documenting the evolution of this unique organizational form in New York.

The product of a cooperative effort by the New York *landsmanshaft* community, the NHPRC, and the YIVO Institute, the *Landsmanshaftn* Archive provides a new resource for examining immigrant social history at the grass-roots level. As the creative response of a mass immigrant population to challenging social and economic conditions, *landsmanshaftn* are a key to understanding the processes of acculturation and immigrant ethnic self-maintenance at work in the settlement of Jewish immigrants in New York.

LANDSMANSHAFTN ARCHIVE: SCOPE AND CONTENT

The *Landsmanshaftn* Archive houses materials from over 800 societies, arranged in 303 record groups. Collections range in size from one folder to 13 feet in length and date from 1859 to 1984. The bulk of the materials were collected between 1979 and 1981.

The types of organizational records contained in the *Landsmanshaftn* Archive consist of: charters; certificates of incorporation; legal documents; constitutions; minutes of regular, special, and executive meetings; financial records, including membership dues books; records of special committees (relief, burial, loan fund, old age, executive, banquet); membership records (applications, lists, cards, censuses); burial records (golden books listing names, dates of death; records of interments, endowments; cemetery maps; burial permits); anniversary celebration and banquet programs, menus, journals, photographs; correspondence; meeting announcements and bulletins; honorary certificates and citations; memorial (*yisker*) books, publication manuscripts and materials; realia; banners; seals; photographs; personal immigration records and papers of society members. Society records, both handwritten and printed, are generally in Yiddish and English; prior to 1950, minutes, were usually recorded in Yiddish, subsequently in English. However, records do exist in both German and Hungarian and collections contain correspondence and printed matter in Polish and Russian.

Finding aids to record groups consist of record group (RG) descriptions which are part of the general YIVO Archives inventory. Record group descriptions are numbered consecutively and detail the major record series within the collections; give donor information; locate the materials in the archives; and outline the history of each society or the individual's organizational activities in the cases of collections of personal papers. These short historical sketches are culled from information provided by *Landsmanshaftn* Project questionnaires completed by society representatives; the records themselves; *The Jewish Landsmanschaften of New York*, published by the Yiddish Writers' Union under the auspices of the Works Progress Administration in 1938 (Yiddish); and *The Jewish Communal Register of New York City, 1917-1918,* published by the Kehillah of New York City, 1918.

Landsmanshaftn materials not comprising individual record groups are arranged alphabetically by the organization's locality or its title's first word in the "Subject Collection: *Landsmanshaftn*" (RG 123) and are listed in Appendix II. Records are available to researchers without restrictions unless otherwise noted.

Minute book, Satanover Unterstitzung Verein, October, 1903. (Donated by the Satanover Benevolent Society)

ORGANIZATION OF THE GUIDE

Section A: Locality-Based Society Records

Section A alphabetically lists by location and describes those collections of societies originally organized on the basis of the place of origin of the founding members. All types of *landsmanshaft* organizational forms are represented: the *khevres* or *ansheys*, societies affiliated with a religious congregation or the religious congregations themselves; independent men's associations and their sister groups, the ladies auxiliaries; branches of Jewish fraternal orders; independent ladies societies; relief groups; *landsmanshaftn* federations. Collections of personal papers relating to locality-based societies are also included in this section. Guide entries summarize the information contained in the YIVO Archives record group descriptions.

Section B: Non-Locality Based Society Records

Section B alphabetically lists by first word of title and describes those mutual-aid organizations, non-geographically delimited, but structurally and in terms of purpose, built on the *landsmanshaft* model. Similarly founded by immigrants, these societies include associations named after individuals; those arbitrarily named; societies organized according to occupation; family circles; congregational benevolent societies. As in Section A, entries summarize YIVO Archives finding aids to the collections.

Sections A & B: Guide Format

MODEL ENTRY

DYATLOVO
(Pol. Zdzieciol; Yid. Zetl)
Baranovichi province,
Belorussian SSR*

1. Collections of locality-based societies are entered consecutively in alphabetical order according to the current place name of their town or city. An asterisk after the place name description indicates that the town or city in question was at some point within the boundaries of a country other than the one listed. Thus a listing for a town which was at one time within the boundaries of the Austro-Hungarian Empire, but which is at the present time within the boundaries of Poland will be marked by an asterisk. Place name

spelling is based on main entry citations in *The Columbia Lippincott Gazeteer**, thus enabling the researcher to find a particular locality on a contemporary map. The terms *"oblast"* and *"województwo"* used in the *Gazeteer* have been translated as "province." Additionally, where variant names and spellings are pertinent in clarifying a society's name or location, these, too, are cited. In Section B, collections are entered consecutively in alphabetical order according to the first word of the society's name or its locality.

56. Independent Zetler Young Men's Benevolent Association. Records, 1920-1973, 1' 9" (RG 824)

2. Entries in both Sections A and B include the entry number; complete name of the organization or collection of personal papers; inclusive dates of the records; size of the collection; record group (RG) number in the YIVO Archives.

Founded in 1904. Established an old age fund, loan fund, and *khevre-kedishe* (burial committee) for its members. Provided relief for *landslayt*** after WWI, including sending a delegate to Zetl. Aided survivors after WWII.

3. Historical notes follow, citing founding dates and special features of each organization's history where available. Information common to all societies, e.g., place of founding, purpose, and activities are *not* repeated in the Guide. Thus, the following can be attributed to each *landsmanshaft* or non-locality based society, unless otherwise indicated: its founding location was New York; its purpose was to provide mutual aid. Functions included burial; payment of sick and death benefits; financial assistance; social activities for members; fund-raising and relief drives.

Constitution; minutes, 1920-42, 1952-57; financial records, 1949-57, 1961-73; golden book (record of deaths of members); photographs; miscellaneous.

4. Descriptions of record groups in both sections cite dates of organizational records, highlighting minutes and financial materials. Records are usually in Yiddish and English; language is noted only when it is other than the above.

The Columbia Lippincott Gazeteer of the World, Columbia University Press, New York, 1970. Where a location could not be found in the *Gazeteer*, other sources were used.
**Fellow countrymen (plural of *landsman* "countryman")

Appendix I: Materials received after the completion of the *Landsmanshaftn* Project.

Appendix II: "Subject Collection: *Landsmanshaftn*" (not indexed) (entry 303, RG 123)

The subject collection contains miscellaneous materials and ephemera from over 500 Jewish mutual-aid societies. These materials are alphabetically listed in the appendix by the society's locality or the first word of its name.

Appendix III: Locations of Jewish cemeteries in New York City and Environs.

Index

Access to individual society records described in the Guide entries is best obtained through the index. Index entries consist of:

1. official names of main entry organizations with pertinent spelling and titular variants;
2. official names of other societies whose records appear as part of collections listed in the Guide;

3. geographic entries under which locality-based societies are listed, with pertinent language and spelling variants.
4. names of fraternal parent organizations to which lodges, branches, or chapters belong.

Thus, the "Henry Clay Lodge No. 15, Independent Order Brith Abraham" (entry #166) and other societies with records included in that collection are entered in the index as follows:

Henry Clay Lodge No. 15, I.O.B.A., 166	(main title entry for society)
Clay, Henry, Lodge No. 15, I.O.B.A., 166	(additional index entry for the above)
Plock, 166, 167	(main geographic entry in Guide; place of origin of members)
Plotsk, 166, 167	(variant spelling of main geographic entry)
Indep. Order Brith Abraham, 166	(fraternal parent organization of Lodge No. 15)
Boris Schatz B.S., Inc., 166	(a society formed by *landslayt* from Plock, with records within the Henry Clay Lodge collection)
Schatz, Boris, B.S., Inc., 166	(additional index entry for the above)

The names and locations of societies and individuals in Appendix I appear in the index. The names and locations of societies in Appendix II, "Subject Collection: *Landsmanshaftn*," do *not* appear in the index.

Charter members, First Independent Storoznetzer Bukowiner Sick and Benevolent Association, established in New York, 1903. (Donated by the First Independent Storoznetzer Bukowiner S.B.A.)

SECTION A: LOCALITY-BASED SOCIETY RECORDS

ALEXANDROVSK
Dnepropetrovsk province,
Ukrainian SSR

1. Friends of Alexandrovsk Benevolent Association, Inc.
Records, 1922, 1926-1979, 10" (RG 843)

Established and incorporated in 1926. Affiliated with the Alexandrowsker Relief, Inc. Activities included maintaining a loan fund; support for Israel. Dissolved June 1979.

Certificates of incorporation: Alexandrowsker Relief, Inc., 1922; Friends of Alexandrovsk B.A., 1926; constitution; minutes, 1926, 1955-79; financial records, 1930's-70's; anniversary journals; materials relating to burial, including a calligraphic *pinkes* (record book); miscellaneous.

ANTOPOL
Brest province,
Belorussian SSR*

2. Antepoler Young Men's Benevolent Association
Records, 1923-1979, 15" (RG 883)

Organized 1906. Activities included establishing a loan fund for its members. A ladies auxiliary was organized in 1913, later disbanded and reorganized in 1929 as the Antepoler Young Ladies Auxiliary. After WWI engaged in relief activities for *landslayt* in Antopol, sending funds to the Antopol talmud torah (free religious school), Tarbut Hebrew schools, the free loan fund.

Constitution of the Antepoler Y.M.B.A.; of the Antepoler Ladies Auxiliary; financial records, 1950's-70's; correspondence, 1960's-70's; anniversary journal; announcements; miscellaneous.

3. Chevra Anshei Antepoler
Records, 1909-1964, 3" (RG 1004)

Founded in 1901; incorporated in 1909. Maintained a synagogue located at 203 Henry Street, New York.

Certificate of incorporation, 1909; minutes, 1929-64; miscellaneous; constitution, Antepolier U.V.; charter, United Antepoler Association, 1909; postcards, Antopol.

**ANYKSCIAI,
ANIKSHCHYAI**
Lithuanian SSR
Lithuanian Republic,
1918-1940

4. Anikster Benevolent Pischei Tshuvo Association, Inc.
Records, 1931-1976, 10" (RG 937)

Established in 1939 upon the consolidation of the Congregation Bnai Pischei Tshuvo Anshei Aniksty and the Anikster Benevolent Association. The congregation was established in 1887 for the purposes of study; to provide cemetary plots; free loans for members; aid rabbi and talmud torah in Anyksciai. Maintained a synagogue at 135 Henry Street, New York. The Anikster B.A. was organized in 1898. Following consolidation the Anikster Benevolent Pischei Tshuvo Assn. managed the synagogue; sold the building in 1965. Dissolved 1976.

Legal documents, 1930's-40's; minutes, 1936-39; financial records, 1940's-70's; meeting announcements; materials pertaining to sale of synagogue; correspondence; materials pertaining to dissolution; seal.

BACAU
Bacau province,
Rumania

5. First Bacauer Sick and Benevolent Association
Records, 1905-1976, 10" (RG 938)

Established in 1903. Also known as the Erster Bacauer Romanischer Kranken Untershtitsung Fareyn, First Bacauer Rumanian American K.U.V. Dissolved 1976.

Constitutions; financial records, 1922-75 (German, English); materials pertaining to burial; correspondence; materials pertaining to 60th anniversary celebration; materials pertaining to dissolution; seal; stamps.

BARLAD, BERLAD
Barlad province,
Rumania

6. Independent Berlader Benevolent Association
Records, 1958-1974, 2½" (RG 949)

Established in 1919. Active until 1975.

Dues ledger; correspondence; meeting notices; miscellaneous.

BARYSH
(Pol. Barysz)
Ternopol province,
Ukrainian SSR*

7. Baryszer Young Men's Benevolent Association, Inc.
Records, 1934-73, 5" (RG 887)

Organized in 1905; incorporated in 1948. Supported Jewish philanthropies. Dissolved 1974.

Membership book; 1934-69; financial records, 1948-73; correspondence.

BELZ
Moldavian SSR
(in Bessarabia)

8. First Belzer Bessarabier Sick Benevolent Association
Records, 1925-1960, 5" (RG 1002)

Founded in 1900 by 28 *landslayt*. Affiliated with the Ladies Auxiliary of the First Belzer Bess. S.B.A., organized 1930; with the Federation of Bessarabian Societies of America, Inc. Dissolved c. 1974.

Souvenir journals, 1925, 1937; film of last banquet, 1960; photograph.

BEREZHANY
(Pol. Brzezany)
Ternopol province,
Ukranian SSR*

9. Congregation Bnei Jacob Anshei Brzezan
   Records, 1903-1975, 21" (RG 885)

Organized in 1894 and incorporated in 1952 to establish a synagogue. Provided relief for *landslayt* after WWI, including sending a delegate to Berezhany.

Financial records, 1930's-60's; membership records, 1903-47; Golden Book of Memories (record of deaths of members); miscellaneous; wooden gavel.

BERSHAD
Vinnitsa province,
Ukrainian SSR

10. Bershader Benevolent Society, Inc.
   Records, 1937-1949, 5" (RG 816)

Founded in 1912 in Brooklyn. Affiliated with the Erste Bershader K.U.V. (est'd 1906); the Bershader Progressive Association (est'd 1934). Organized the Bershader Relief after WWI; the Relief was reactivated during WWII.

Constitution; minutes of Bershader Book Committee, 1944, 1946; memorial booklet on Bershad; correspondence; anniversary journals; miscellaneous materials collected by donor on the history of Jews in the Ukraine; on Lomazer, Shumsker, and Soroker *landsmanshaftn*.

BESHENKOVICHI
Vitebsk province,
Belorussian SSR

See Chasnick-Bieshenkowitz Society, entry 38.

(Donated by the Kolomear Friends Association)

BESSARABIA
now region of
SW European USSR.

Ballot of the Erste Bolshowcer Kranken Unterstitzung Verein and Lodge 517, Independent Order Brith Abraham, 1926. (Donated by the Ershte Bolshowcer Sick Benefit Society)

11. Bessarabian Federation of American Jews, Inc.
Records, 1940-1950, 5″ (RG 1028)

Originally organized in 1940 as the United Bessarabian Federation; incorporated in 1942 as the Federation of Bessarabian Societies of America, Inc. In 1944 changed name to Bessarabian Federation of American Jews, Inc. Aimed to coordinate relief efforts of independent Bessarabian *landsmanshaftn* in America for residents of Bessarabia and Bessarabian refugees to the United States. Special projects supported Bessarabian orphans in France; building of housing project in Israel. Affiliated with a women's division. Dissolved in the early 1950's.

Materials pertaining to the United Bessarabian Federation, including resolutions, bulletins; materials pertaining to the Federation of Bessarabian Societies of America, including certificate of incorporation, 1942; constitution; financial and relief work records; membership and mailing lists; correspondence; lists and materials of affiliated organizations; photographs.

12. Bessarabier Podolier Benevolent Society, Inc.
Records, 1933-1974, 5″ (RG 1024)

Founded in 1954 by former members of the Jewish People's Fraternal Order (J.P.F.O.) of the International Workers' Order (I.W.O.) when the latter order was dissolved during the McCarthy era. In 1930, a group of members of the Zwanitz-Podolier Br. 277 Workmen's Circle broke away to join the I.W.O. as its Branch 277. This branch merged with another Workmen's Circle branch to form the Podolier Br. 277 I.W.O., later affiliating with yet another branch, renaming itself the Baltic Podolier Br. 277 I.W.O. Was affiliated with the Emma Lazarus Club #277 I.W.O. Some of the members of Branch 277 supported the Zwanitz-Podolier Relief Committee. In 1954, members of branch 277 formed the East Bronx Cultural Society. This later merged with the former Bessarabier Br. 302 I.W.O. to form the Bessarabier Podolier B.S., Inc.

Records of the Bessarabier Podolier B.S., Inc.: minutes, 1958-60; financial papers; anniversary journals; photographs; of the East Bronx Cultural Society (photocopies): certificate of incorporation, 1955; constitution; minutes; of the Baltic Podolier Br. 277 I.W.O.: speeches, meeting announcements; anniversary journal; photographs; of the Podolier Br. 277 I.W.O., including "wall newspapers," 1932-40's; of the Bessarabier Br. 302 I.W.O., including minutes, 1943-47; personal papers of donor; miscellaneous; photograph.

13. National Council for Bessarabian Jews
Records, 1950-1972, 2″ (RG 1029)

Organized in 1950 as a division of the Histadrut campaign in America. Was affiliated with Histadrut Haovdim and the National Committee for Labor Israel. Many members were formerly associated with the Bessarabian Federation of American Jews, Inc.

Minutes, 1950-51; bulletins, 1950's-60's; publications; publications of the World Federation of Bessarabian Jews, 1960's-70's; photograph album of the First World Conference of Bessarabian Jews, 1958; miscellaneous, including list of Bessarabian WWII survivors.

14. Schwartz, Rose (1900-   )
   Papers, 1940-1974, 15" (RG 1000)

Born in Kishinev, Bessarabia in 1900. Emigrated to U.S., 1920. Was active member of the Federation of Bessarabian Societies of America, Inc. and vice-president of its Women's Division; served as vice-president of the Bessarabian Federation of American Jews. Affiliated with the Bronx Bessarabier Br. 302 International Workers' Order and was a founder of its Women's Club. Also became a member of the Bessarabier Podolier Benevolent Society. Worked for the Jewish Council for Russian War Relief and the American Society for Russian War Relief, Inc.

Correspondence, 1940-74; reports; materials pertaining to Bessarabian Jews in France, 1940's-50's (French Russian, Yiddish); scrapbook; newspaper clippings; honorary citations pertaining to R.S.'s life and organizational activities; photographs; publications of the Federation of Bessarabian Societies, Inc.; Bessarabian Federation of American Jews; Bessarabier Podolier B.S.; Federation of Bessarabian Jews in Israel, 1940's-50's; miscellaneous publications.

A note of thanks to Rose Schwartz written on a photograph of the young residents of an orphanage in Paris which she later visited as an emissary of the World Federation of Bessarabian Jews, 1946. (Donated by Rose Schwartz)

BIECZ
(Yid. Beytch)
Rzeszow province, Poland

15. First Beitcher Sick Benevolent Society
Records, 1929-1979, 17½" (RG 772)

Organized in 1903 to send relief to Biecz after a fire; chartered later that year. Affiliated with the Beitcher Sisterhood and Young Beitcher Social League. Aided *landslayt* in Biecz after WWI and WWII. Established a free loan society for *landslayt* in Israel.

Constitution; minutes, 1929-42; financial records, 1969-72, 1977; relief work records, 1940-62; membership applications; bulletins, 1949-79; correspondence; memorial book, 1960; photographs.

BIELSK PODLASKI
Bialystok province, Poland

16. Bielsker Bruderlicher Untershtitzungs Verein
Records, 1924-1949, 1975, 3" (RG 1046)

Founded in 1888. Established a loan fund, 1902; old age and disability relief fund, 1921. Affiliated with the United Bielsker Relief which aided *landslayt* in Israel. Associated with a ladies auxiliary.

Anniversary souvenir journals, 1924, 28, 38, 48; membership directory, 1949; correspondence; memorial book, 1975.

BIRCZA
Rzeszow province, Poland

17. Birczer Young Men's Benevolent Society
Records, 1926-1954, 5" (RG 1003)

Founded in 1897 with 30 members. Established old age and loan funds for members.

Constitution; minutes, 1925-54 (Yiddish/German written in Roman alphabet); miscellaneous, including letter from artisans' union in Bircza, 1926.

BOBRUISK, BOBRUYSK
Bobruisk province, Belorussian SSR

18. Reuben Guskin Babroisker Branch 206 Workmen's Circle
Records, 1958-1977, 2" (RG 812)

Founded in 1908 as the Babroisker Branch of the Workmen's Circle. Renamed for Reuben Guskin, organizational leader and *landsman*, after his death in 1962. Activities included establishment of a relief committee after WWI; publication of a memorial book together with *landslayt* in Israel after WWII.

Minutes, 1958-77.

BOGOPOL
Odessa province, Ukrainian SSR

19. Bogopoler Unterstutzungs Verein
Records, 1917-1975, 5" (RG 895)

Founded in 1893 by 11 *landslayt*. Established a *gmiles-khesed* (free loan) fund to aid needy members. Sent relief to Bogopol during WWI and WWII.

Constitution; minutes, 1943-63; financial records, 1930's-60's; membership records; materials pertaining to burial, including 3 cemetery maps, 1925-73; materials pertaining to anniversary celebrations, including souvenir journals; meeting announcements, 1940's-70's.

BOLSHOVTSY
(Pol. Bolszowce)
Stanislav province,
Ukrainian SSR*

20. Ershte Bolshowcer Sick Benevolent Society and Lodge No. 517 Independent Order Brith Abraham
Records, 1909-1930, 5" (RG 872)

Lodge No. 517 was founded as the Ershte Bolszowcer Arbeiter Lodge No. 517 I.O.B.A. The Ershte Bolshowcer S.B.S. was founded c. 1909 as a mutual-aid society. The two affiliated c. 1924.

Minutes of the Lodge No. 517, 1909-23; of the S.B.S. and Lodge, 1925-30; miscellaneous, including bulletin of the Chevra Rodfey Tsedek Anshei Bolszowce, 1930's.

BORISLAV
(Pol. Boryslaw)
Drogobych province,
Ukrainian SSR*

See Chevra Gomle Chesed Anshe Drohobych and Boryslaw, entry 53.

BOTOSANI, BOTOSHANI
Botosani province,
Rumania

21. United Botoshaner American Brotherly and Benevolent Association
Records, 1916-1973, 5" (RG 877)

Incorporated in 1904 and reorganized in 1906. Activities included the financial support of charitable institutions and the State of Israel.

Minutes, 1957-65; financial records, 1953-66; membership applications, 1940-71; correspondence, 1950's-73; cemetery materials, 1916-64.

BRANSK
(Rus. Bryansk)
Bialystok province,
Poland

22. Brainsker Brothers Aid Society
Records, 1924-1971, 2½" (RG 980)

Founded in 1894. Provided members with a loan fund. Active until 1979.

Minutes, 1963-71; materials pertaining to burial; anniversary journal.

BRATISLAVA
(Ger. Pressburg)
Bratislava province,
Czechoslovakia

23. First Pressburger Sick and Benevolent Society
Records, 1906-1974, 10" (RG 854)

Dissolved in the 1970's; no further information available.

Financial records, 1948-74; membership application book, 1906-51 (German, English); burial permits, 1914-73; correspondence, 1950's-70's.

BRATSLAV
Vinnitsa province,
Ukrainian SSR

24. First Bratslow Podolier Sick Benefit Society
Records, 1915-1944, 15" (RG 836)

Founded in 1914. Established a relief committee during WWI.

Constitution; minutes, 1915-20; minutes of relief fund, 1944; membership dues records, 1925-42; membership loan information, 1927-44; financial materials; gavel.

25. First Bratslower Ladies Auxiliary
Records, 1934-61, 5" (RG 835)

A ladies auxiliary affiliated with the First Bratslow Podolier S.B.S. Participated with that society in a relief fund, 1940's.

Minutes, 1933-36, 1938-44; financial/membership records, 1930's-50's; gavel.

BREST
(Yid. Brisk,
Pol. Brisi nad Bugie)
Brest-Litovsk,
Brest province,
Belorussian SSR*

26. United Brisker Relief
Records, 1916-1978, 13" (RG 898)

Established in 1915 by a group of Brisker societies to aid the war-stricken community of Brisk. Undertook large-scale relief and rehabilitation work between WWI and II. Located and sent relief to refugees and survivors of WWII; supported the Palestine *yishuv* (settlement) and the State of Israel. Maintained branches in Newark, Detroit, Chicago, Cleveland, Los Angeles. Active until 1978.

Statistics and official reports, including data gathered in Brisk; correspondence: from organizations, institutions in Brisk, 1919-39; with members, committees, affiliated groups, 1920-65; with national Jewish organizations, 1919-73; regarding activities in Palestine/Israel, 1947-73; meeting notices, 1916-78; scrapbook including photographs of relief activities in Brisk; historical memoirs; materials pertaining to publication of memorial book; memorial book, 1954; records of affiliated organizations: Brisker and Vicinity Aid Society of Los Angeles, Agudas Achim Aid Society.

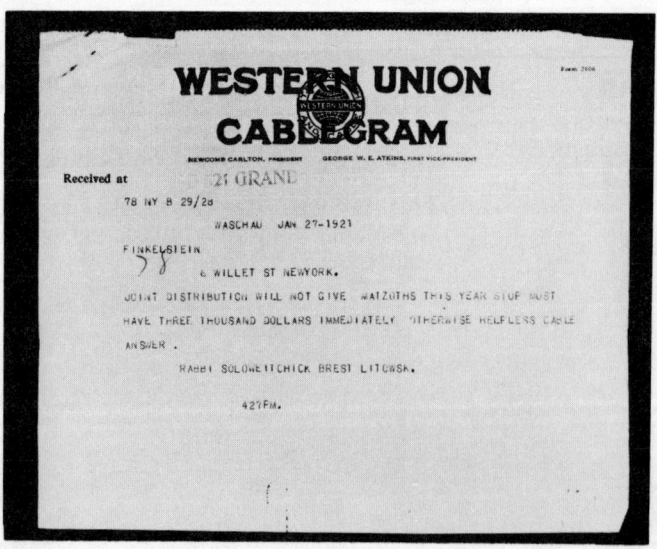

Telegram sent to Jacob Finkelstein, secretary of the United Brisker Relief, from Rabbi Soloweitchik in Brisk. (Donated by the United Brisker Relief)

BRICHANY
(Rum. Briceni)
Moldavian SSR
(in Bessarabia)

27. First Britchaner Benevolent Association, Inc.
Records, 1932-1977, 22½" (RG 973)

Established in 1895. Organized free loan fund in 1925; old age fund in 1935. Affiliated with the Britchaner Bessarabian Relief Assn. Dissolved 1977.

By-laws; minutes, 1932-77; financial records, 1936-70's; materials pertaining to old age and loan funds; golden book (record of deaths of members); membership records; materials pertaining to cemetery and burial; miscellaneous; seal; stamp.

28. Kessler, Joseph (1891-1979)
Papers, 1935-1979, 10" (RG 1001)

Born in Brichany in 1891. Emigrated to U.S., 1910. Served as president of the Britchaner Bessarabian Relief Assn.; honorary president, Britchaner Relief in Israel; chairman, Workmen's Circle Histadrut Division. Died in the Bronx, N.Y., 1979.

Financial papers; correspondence with Britchaner Relief in Israel, 1950's-60's; souvenir journals, Britchaner Bessarabian Relief, 1937-41, 1946; publications: Workmen's Circle Division of the National Committee for Labor Israel, United Organizations for Israel Histadrut; photographs; miscellaneous.

BROOKLYN
New York

29. Borough of Brooklyn Lodge
Records, 1933-1965, 3" (RG 947)

Founded in 1898. Benefits included loans for members. Dissolved 1965.

Rules and by-laws; financial records; loan fund materials; cemetery records; correspondence; seal.

30. Israelite Fraternity of Brooklyn, Inc.
Records, 1961-1973, 2½" (RG 1006)

Established in Brooklyn, date unknown. Dissolved in the 1970's.

Financial records; address book; seal.

BRZEZINY
(Rus. Breziny)
Lodz province, Poland

31. Breziner Sick and Benevolent Society, Inc.
Records, 1908-1976, 10" (RG 809)

Founded, 1896 and chartered in 1899. Established the Breziner Ladies Auxiliary, 1932; the Breziner Relief Committee, 1945. Maintains ties and conducts joint activities with the Breziner *landsmanshaft* in Israel.

Constitution; minutes, 1953-70; financial records pertaining to relief activities in Poland, Germany, Israel; correspondence pertaining to WWII relief activities, 1941-76; untitled manuscript of Jacob Fogel's memoirs of Brzeziny; anniversary journals; newspaper clippings; photographs; miscellaneous membership records; materials pertaining to memorial book.

BUCHACH
(Pol. Buczacz)
Ternopol province,
Ukrainian SSR*

32. Buczacz-American Benevolent Sick and Aid Society
Records, 1921-1960, 5" (RG 844)

Founded in 1905. Affiliated with the United Buczaczer Ladies Auxiliary; First Buczaczer Society, Circle of Buczaczer Friends. Circle of Buczaczer Friends organized in 1942, growing out of the Betshutsher Literarishn Fareyn (Buczaczer Literary Union), founded in 1916, later reorganizing in 1921 as the Betshutsher Literarishn Klub. It provided social, educational, and cultural activities for members, publishing a humorous newspaper read aloud at meetings. The Circle dissolved in 1970.

Constitution; minutes, 1937-48 (German, English); financial records, 1942-58; *Betshutsher nudnik*, handwritten Yiddish newspaper, 3 issues, 1921-22; materials pertaining to the Circle of Buczaczer Friends; photographs; miscellaneous.

BUCHAREST
Rumania

33. Independent Bukarester Sick Aid Association
Records, 1901-1976, 2'7" (RG 826)

Founded in 1901; incorporated in 1910. Activities included establishment of a loan fund, 1914; a ladies auxiliary, 1931; a relief fund, 1932; an old age fund, 1933. Merged with the Independent Young Men's Roumanian Benevolent Association, 1931. Supported HIAS in relief activities after WWII; now support Israel.

Constitutions; minutes, 1949-62, 1963-66; financial records; membership records, including registration book, 1901-25 (German, English); correspondence; souvenir journals; miscellaneous materials.

BUDANOV
(Pol. Budzanow)
Ternopol province,
Ukrainian SSR*

34. Erste Budzanower Kranken Untershtitsung Verein
Records, 1929-1946, 1971, 2½" (RG 997)

Established in 1895. Activities included establishment of a synagogue. Supported a talmud torah (free religious school) in Budanov.

Minutes, 1929-40, 1971; golden book (record of deaths of members); free loan record book; souvenir journal; memoirs of Budanov.

BURDUJENI
Suceava province,
Rumania

35. Independent Burdujener Sick and Benevolent Society
Records, 1938-1976, 10" (RG 853)

Organized in 1906. Activities included establishment of a free loan fund for members; support for Israel. Dissolved 1976.

Minutes, 1938-40, 1947-76; financial records, 1930's-70's; burial permits; seal.

BUSKO
(Rus. Busk)
Kielce province,
Poland

36. Busker Bnai Brith Sick and Benevolent Association
Records, 1947-1967, 5½" (RG 810)

Founded in 1911. Activities included the establishment of a *shtibl* (Hasidic synagogue), 1911-35; a *gmiles-khesed* (free loan fund). Sent relief to Busk; organized a free loan society there before WWII. Aided *landslayt* in Poland and Israel after WWII. Maintain contact with the Busker *landsmanshaft* in Israel.

Constitution; minutes, 1947-62; correspondence; *yortsayt* book (commemorative volume); photographs; memorial book, 1965; anniversary journals, including those of the New York-Boston Busker Relief Association, Busker Orphan Asylum Foundation; materials pertaining to the *landsmanshaft* in Israel, including statutes, 1957; miscellaneous.

CAUCASUS, CAUCASIA
USSR

37. Caucasian Benevolent Society, Inc.
Records, 1932-1974, 8" (RG 890)

Founded in 1924. Maintained a loan fund; sent relief funds to the Caucasus, Birobidzhan (USSR), and Israel. Affiliated with a ladies auxiliary.

Certificate of incorporation, 1924; minutes, 1970-72; financial records, 1930's-70's; membership records, 1950's-70's; correspondence; anniversary materials; banner.

CHASHNIKI
Vitebsk province,
Belorussian SSR

38. Chasnick-Bieshenkowitzer Society
Records, 1958-1975, 10½" (RG 886)

Organized in 1898 as the Chasnek-Bieshinkovicher Verein. Dissolved in the 1970's. Activities included support for charitable institutions and Israel.

Minutes, 1966-75; financial records, 1958-75; membership records, 1958-75; miscellaneous; seal.

CHAUSSY
Mogilev province,
Belorussian SSR

39. Tchausser Society
Records, 1924-1959, 2½" (RG 983)

Incorporated in the Bronx in 1924 to promote friendship among members; and to spread American ideals among members and foreigners and foreign-born citizens. Provided medical and death benefits. Dissolved, date unknown.

Certificate of incorporation, 1924; constitution; minutes, 1925-59; materials pertaining to burial; miscellaneous.

CHECHELNIK
Vinnitsa province,
Ukrainian SSR

40. Chechelnicker Benevolent Association of Greater New York, Inc.
Records, 1958-1971, 2½" (RG 1054)

Founded in 1928. Built community center in Lydda, Israel through the United Jewish Appeal.

Constitution; receipts; correspondence; photographs; memoirs of donor; certificate.

CHERKASSY
Kiev province,
Ukrainian SSR

41. Cherkasser-Smela Benevolent Association, Inc.
Records, 1910-1963, 7½" (RG 786)

Formed in 1962 through the consolidation of the United Brothers of the Town of Smila (incorporated 1906) and the Cherkasser Benevolent Assn. (incorporated 1945); The United Brothers established the Relief Committee for the Smeler Political Convicts, 1913; the Joint Smeler Relief, Inc., 1928. Relief activities included establishing a barrel factory and woodwork factory in Smela, 1930.

Minutes, United Brothers Town of Smila, 1932-43; certificate of consolidation, 1962; correspondence from Smela to the N.Y. *landsmanshaft* and to the Smiller B.A. in Philadelphia, 1910-14, 1922, 1931-32; lists of relief packages received in the USSR, 1922, 1942-48; newspaper clippings; notes in preparation of Smeler memorial book; souvenir journal of the Joint Smela Relief, Inc., 1928; receipts from the Hilfs Committee for the Smela Political Convicts.

Letter, 1920's, from children in orphanage in Smela, the Ukraine, which was sponsored by the Cherkasser-Smela Benevolent Association, Inc. in New York.

"Dear friends in America,
We children who find ourselves in the Smeler Children's Home thank you for the food and for the clothes and shoes. We children from the Smeler Children's Home ask you not to forget us in the future."
(Donated by the Cherkasser-Smela Benevolent Association, Inc.)

**CHERNOVTSY,
CZERNOWITZ**
Chernovtsy province,
Ukrainian SSR
(in Bukovina)

42. United Friends of Czernowitz
    Records, 1941-1973, 3" (RG 1062)

Founding date of society unknown. Dissolved 1970's.

Financial records, 1941-73; membership dues book, 1940's-73.

CHERVEN
(until 1920's, Igumen)
Minsk province,
Belorussian SSR

43. Igumener Independent Benevolent Association
    Records, 1913-1974, 5" (RG 893)

Founded in 1899 to promote "unity and brotherly friendship." Provided loans for its members and retained the services of a doctor. Attempted to send a delegate with funds to Igumen after the 1917 Russian Revolution. In 1978, the society's president visited Igumen and distributed funds there.

Constitution; minutes, 1919-39; photographs.

CHERVONOARMEISK
(until 1940, Radzivilov,
Pol. Radziwillow)
Rovno province,
Ukrainian SSR*

44. Radziviller-Woliner Benevolent Association
    Records, 1929-1962, 3" (RG 951)

Organized in 1916. Provided a loan fund for members. During and between the two world wars had a relief committee which aided Radzivilov and refugees.

Correspondence; souvenir journals; visual materials pertaining to the *lines-hatsedek* (hospital committee) in Radzivilov, including photographs and hand-painted cards.

CHMIELNIK
Kielce province,
Poland

45. Chmielniker Sick and Benevolent Society
    Records, 1935-1978, 8" (RG 1081)

Organized in 1929 as the Chmielniker Sick and Benevolent Society of Poland, Inc. Conducted relief drives during WWII. Financially aided *landslayt* in Israel after the war. Chmielniker Young Ladies Auxiliary established in 1931 to aid needy *landslayt* and charitable institutions.

Souvenir journal, 1935; journal of the United Chmielniker Relief Committee, 1938; meeting notices; journal of the Association of Former Residents of Chmielnik in Israel, 1963, 1967-76, 1978; photographic plate; stamp; banners; cemetery map; memorial book, 1960.

CZESTOCHOWA
Formerly Kielce province,
Poland

46. United Czenstochower Relief Committee
Records, 1925, 1941-1964, 20" (RG 987)

Organized in 1914 to help *landslayt* in need, sickness; to create jobs for immigrants. Formally named the United Czenstochower Relief Committee in 1921. Under the leadership of labor leader Raphael Federman, Relief president, located and supported surviving *landslayt* scattered worldwide after WWII; aided them in searching for relatives. Published two memorial books. Now merged with the Chenstochauer Young Men, Inc. Thirteen *landsmanshaftn* from the provinces of Kielce and Lodz worked with the Relief.

Minutes, 1948-55; financial records, 1944-49; correspondence: requests for assistance sent by *landslayt* and societies in Australia, Italy, Germany, Czestochowa, Israel, Austria, Poland, France, Belgium, North and South America, Cuba, Sweden; correspondence of Raphael Federman; with Jewish committees in Displaced Persons Camps; scrapbook of newspaper clippings relating to events in Czestochowa and relief activities; meeting announcements; bulletins; materials pertaining to anniversary, liberation, and Raphael Federman Jubilee celebrations; miscellaneous, including testimony against a Nazi officer of the Czestochowa ghetto, 1959 (German); materials of affiliated Czestochower societies in the U.S.: Czenstochover Club, Chenstochover Lodge 11, International Workers' Order, Czenstochauer B.V. & U.V., Czenstochauer Young Men, Inc.

DABIE
(Rus. Dombe)
Lodz province, Poland

47. Dombier Benevolent Society
Records, 1880's, 1913-1939, 5½" (RG 781)

Organized in 1916. Merged with the Kladowa Society in 1970.

Constitution; minutes, 1916-22; personal materials and photographs pertaining to the Kash family in Dabie and the in U.S., 1913-39; pall cloth.

DEBICA, DEMBICA
Rzeszow province,
Poland

48. Dembitzer Landsleit, Inc.
Records, 1953-1974, 2½" (RG 1047)

Established in 1950 and incorporated in 1955 to unite all former reisdents of Dembica to "revive and uphold the traditions of our Dembitzer birthplace through social, cultural, non-political means." Assisted in the publication of a memorial book.

Certificate of incorporation, 1955; constitution; minutes, 1953-70; bulletins; memorial book, 1960; miscellaneous.

DELATYCZE
Nowogrodek province,
Belorussian SSR*

49. Delatizer Aid Benevolent Society
Records, 1932-1974, 5" (RG 889)

Established in 1905. Maintained a *khevre-kedishe* (burial committee); established a society loan fund, 1914. Merged with a progressive Delatizer society in the 1930's.

Constitution; financial records, 1932-71; meeting announcements; miscellaneous, including constitution of the Drisser Brothers B.S.

DIMER
Kiev province, USSR

50. First Dimerer Progressive Society
Records, 1925-1950, 1½" (RG 1007)

Organized in 1919. Maintained a loan association. Helped members serving in the U.S. armed forces during WWII.

Amendments to constitution, 1950; minutes, 1939-43; dues records, 1925-32; miscellaneous.

DINOVITZ
Kamenets-Podolski province, Ukrainian SSR

51. First Progressive Ladies of Dinewitz
Records, 1945-1967, 2½" (RG 870)

A women's mutual-aid society providing sick and death benefits to members. Dissolved 1967.

Minutes, 1945-66; financial records, 1950's-60's; correspondence, 1950's-60's.

DISNA
(Pol. Dzisna)
Polotsk province, Belorussian SSR

52. United Disner Benevolent Association
Records, 1923-1977, 2½" (RG 795)

Founded and chartered in 1923 to assist *landslayt* in Disna. Published a memorial book in Israel.

Constitutions; minutes, 1939, 1942-60; membership lists; announcements, 1923-61; invitations, 1961-77; newspaper clippings; memorial book, 1969.

DROGOBYCH
(Pol. Drohobycz)
Drogobych province, Ukrainian SSR*

53. Chevra Gomle Chesed Anshe Drohobych and Boryslaw
Records, 1940-1975, 5" (RG 936)

Founded in 1905 as a religious congregation. Activities included establishment of a synagogue; aiding *landslayt* in Drohobycz.

Financial records, 1940's-70's; materials pertaining to burial; seal.

DUBOY
Pinsk county, Minsk province, Belorussian SSR

54. Duboier Young Men's Progressive Association, Inc.
Records, 1938-1979, 5" (RG 1022)

Founded in 1928 at the wedding of a *landsman* from Duboy.

Minutes, 1939-58; anniversary journal; meeting announcements, 1938-79, including those of the Duboier Young Ladies Club, 1940's.

Black and yellow metal shield of Congregation Bnei Aharon Anshei Wilkomir (sic)

DUKLA
Rzeszow province,
Poland

55. Duklar Relief Society, Inc.
Records, 1944-1968, 2½" (RG 799)

Organized in 1920 for relief purposes; incorporated in 1923. Aided *landslayt* in Europe and Israel after WWII. Dissolved in the 1970's.

Minutes, 1948-58; financial records, 1955-58; correspondence, 1951-68; membership lists; news clippings.

DYATLOVO
(Pol. Zdzieciol; Yid. Zetl)
Baranovichi province,
Belorussian SSR*

56. Independent Zetler Young Men's Benevolent Association
Records, 1920-1973, 1'9" (RG 824)

Founded in 1904. Established an old age fund, a loan fund, and a *khevre-kedishe* (burial committee) for members. Provided relief for *landslayt* after WWI, including sending a delegate to Zetl; aided survivors after WWII.

Constitution; minutes, 1920-42, 1952-57; financial records, 1949-57, 1961-73; golden book (record of deaths of members); photographs; miscellaneous.

DZHURIN
Vinnitsa province,
Ukrainian SSR

57. First Djouriner Podolier Alliance, Inc.
Records, 1915-1979, 5" (RG 892)

Founded by twenty *landslayt* in 1915. The constitution states that the question of affiliating with a synagogue should never be brought up. Society provided a loan fund for membership. Ladies Committee of the society sponsored relief activities during WWII.

Constitution; minutes, 1915-25; financial records, 1950's-70's; anniversary journal; meeting announcements; photograph; miscellaneous; gavel.

FASTOV
Kiev province,
Ukrainian SSR

58. United Fastoffer No. 1, Inc.
Records, 1929-1968, 15½" (RG 874)

Founded in 1900 as the United Congregation Anshe Fastoff Independent No. 1. Its activities included the establishment of a synagogue. Subsequently, the society became more secular and was renamed the United Fastoffer No. 1, Inc. A ladies auxiliary existed until 1969.

Financial records, 1914-27, 1940's-1960's; membership records, 1920's-60's; correspondence, 1930's-40's; miscellaneous.

GABIN
(Rus. Gombin)
Warszawa province,
Poland

59. Gombiner Young Men's Benevolent Association, Inc.
Records, 1926, 1952-1979, 10" (RG 842)

Established in 1923 to help bring *landslayt* from Gombin to the U.S. Affiliated with the Gombiner Relief Committee, Gombiner Lending Society, Gombiner Ladies Auxiliary. American Gombiner societies joined to build the Gombiner House in Israel; to establish a loan fund for *landslayt* there; to publish a memorial book.

Constitution; minutes, 1952-77; financial records, 1967-79; photographs; memorial book, 1951; miscellaneous.

GALICIA *Historical region consisting of the territories incorporated into Austria in 1772 at the time of the first partition of Poland. The capital of the region was Lemberg (Lwow). Galicia was included in the boundaries of the second Polish republic (1918-1939); Eastern Galicia, including the former capital Lemberg, is since in the boundaries of the Soviet Union (Ukrainian SSR).*

60. Samaritan Society
Records, 1868-1961, 5" (RG 583)

Founded in 1868 as the Erster Galizischer Kranken und Unterstutzungs Verein. Adopted a constitution in 1872. Later changed name to Samaritan Society.

Membership initiation book, containing: constitution and by-laws, 1872 (German, English); minutes, 1868-77 (German); membership application forms, 1872-97 (German), 1897-1961 (German, English).

61. Workmen's Circle Branch 42
Records, 1911-1955, 5" (RG 923)

Established in 1903 as the Estreicher Arbeiter Bildungs Verein by workers from a variety of towns in the region of Galicia. Activities were cultural and social. Conducted relief work for Jews in Europe during both world wars and in the intervening years.

Minutes, 1900's-1955; anniversary journal.

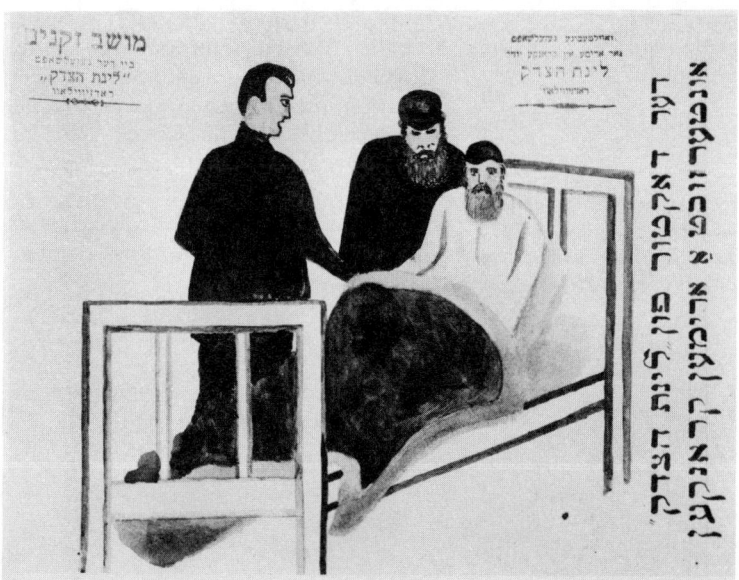

The doctor from the hospital committee visiting a poor, sick patient. (Donated by the Radziviller-Woliner Benevolent Association)

GERMANY

62. The Ceres Union
Records, 1858-1973, 8' 7" (RG 919)

Founded in 1858 as the Ceres Lodge No. 5, United Order Sons of Moses. Organized largely by German Jewish immigrants. After 1861 many members enlisted in the 6th Regiment of the National Guard of the State of New York; three became officers. Established as an independent organization in 1863; changed name to the Ceres Union. Associated with the Yorkville Ceres Club, Ceres Frauen Verein, Ceres Sewing Club, Ceres Council, 1890. Began publication of monthly bulletin "The Ceres Union" in 1905. Affiliated with the Ceres Junior League, 1922; Ceres Union Ladies Auxiliary, established 1931. Dissolved 1973.

Legal documents, 1926, 1973; constitutions; minutes, 1859-64 (German), 1920-72 (English); financial records, 1920's-70's; materials related to membership, 1876-94 (German), 1900's-70's (English); burial and endowments records, 1860-1973; records relating to payment of sick benefits; materials pertaining to anniversary celebrations, 1923-63; "The Ceres Union," monthly bulletin, 1900's-70's; correspondence; photographs; seal.

GORODENKA
(Pol. Horodenka)
Stanislav province,
Ukrainian SSR*

63. Progressive Horodenker Benevolent Society, Inc.
Records, 1914-1979, 20" (RG 820)

Founded in 1914 as the Progressive Horodenker Young Men's and Ladies Sick Benevolent Society, Inc. Formed a joint relief organization after WWI with the First Horodenker Society and the Horodenker Lodge, Indep. Order Brith Abraham. Organized a ladies auxiliary, 1940; its own relief committee, 1944. Also organized a junior league for children of members, 1935. Name changed to Progressive Horodenker B.S., Inc., 1961. Collaborated with *landsmanshaft* in Israel to publish memorial book. Affiliated with Horodenka Friendship Club of Toronto, founded 1972.

Certificate of change of name, 1961; constitution; minutes, 1914-53; financial reports, 1975-77; anniversary journals, including those of the United Horodenker Relief Committee, 1948; First Horodenker S.B.S., 1965, 1970; correspondence; newsletter, 1941-64, 1966; meeting announcements; memoirs and history of society; photographs; memorial book, 1963; miscellaneous.

From a membership application book of the Ceres Union, 1876. (Donated by the State of New York Insurance Department)

GORODISHCHE
(Pol. Horodyszcze)
Baranovichi province,
Belorussian SSR*

64. Horodishter Korsoner Lodge, Inc.
Records, 1930-1974, 10" (RG 855)

Founding date unknown. Dissolved in the 1970's.

Minutes, 1951-59; financial/membership records, 1930-70; correspondence, 1940's-70's.

GRODNO
Grodno province,
Belorussian SSR*

65. Grodner-Lipkaner Branch 74, Workmen's Circle
Records, 1919-1964, 20" (RG 782)

Established through a merger of the Grodner and Lipkaner branches of the Workmen's Circle, 1973. The Grodner branch was originally established as the Grodno Revolutionary Untershtitsung Fareyn. Chartered and joined the Workmen's Circle, 1906. Activities included the formation of the United Grodner Relief, 1915.

Minutes, including dues and expenses records, 1930's-60's; financial records, including records from Grodno, 1919-60's; correspondence; bulletins; notices; ballots; newsletters; anniversary journals, 1926, 1947, 1950, 1956; photographs.

66. Congregation Achei Grodno Vasapotkin and Chevra Mishnayos
Records, 1938-1959, 2½" (RG 995)

The Chevra Mishnayos was established for the daily study of the six volumes of the Mishnah (part of the Talmud). Affiliated with Cong. Achei Grodno Vasapotkin, established by the merger of Cong. Achei Grodno, founded 1893; and Cong. Achei Sapotkin, founded 1913.

Constitution, Chevra Mishnayos; minutes, Chevra Mishnayos, 1938-59; souvenir journal.

(Donated by the Independent Zetler Young Men's Benevolent Association)

67. United Grodner Relief
Records, 1928-1967, 1979-1980, 2½" (RG 996)

Founded in 1915 through the Grodner Branch 74, Workmen's Circle to aid institutions and *landslayt* in Grodno. Sent relief after WWII to surviving *landslayt* in Europe and Israel. Held memorial meetings for Holocaust victims. Affiliated organizations included: Ladies Club of Grodner Br. 74, W.C., Grodner Br. 74, W.C., Friends of Grodno, Novodworer-Grodner Br. 637, W.C., Indep. Grodner S.S.S., Cong. Rabeinu Nochum Anshei Grodno, Grodner Aid B.A. of Brooklyn, Sisterhood of Grodno.

Minutes, 1935-47; publications, 1940's; meeting notices, 1938-67, 1979-80; materials of other Grodner societies: Ind. Grodno S.S.S., Sisterhood of Grodno; Cong. Anshei Grodno, Grodner Patronat, Grodno of Philadelphia Lodge 259, Ind. Order Brith Abraham, Grodner Club, Grodner Relief Alliance of the U.S. and Canada, Friends of Grodno.

GRODZISK, GRODZISK MAZOWIECKI
Warszawa province, Poland

68. Grodzisker Mutual Aid Society
Records, 1926-1963, 2½" (RG 1010)

First established in 1911; reestablished, 1913. Was affiliated with the Junior Grodzisker Mutual Aid Society, Grodzisker Ladies Auxiliary. Formed relief committee, 1938.

Anniversary journals, 1920's-60's; meeting announcement; photograph.

GUSYATIN
(Pol. Husiatyn)
Ternopol province, Ukrainian SSR*

69. Husiatyner-Podolier Friendship Circle
Records, 1961-1977, 2½" (RG 1055)

Founded in 1950. Women formed a ladies auxiliary first, then about 100 *landslayt* all met together to form the Circle. Built a kindergarten, trade school in Israel; support charities.

Minutes, 1971, 1977; correspondence; photographs; memorial book, 1968; miscellaneous.

HUNGARY

70. Central Hungarian Sick Benevolent and Literary Society
Records, 1941-1975, 5" (RG 989)

Established in 1904/6. Contributed to Jewish charities. Supported Israel. Dissolved 1979.

Minutes, 1941-72 (Hungarian, English); financial records; burial and monument permits.

71. Kossuth Association of New York, Inc.
Records, 1930-1971, 6" (RG 906)

Founded in 1904 by Hungarian Jewish immigrants. Society originally named Kossuth Ferencz Literary Sick and Benevolent Association after the son of Kossuth Lajos and president of the Hungarian Party of Independence. Incorporated in 1934.

Financial records, 1947-71; anniversary journals, 1930, 1939, 1954 (Hungarian, English).

72. Pannonia Lodge No. 185, Independent Order of Odd Fellows
Records, 1920-1963, 2'2" (RG 869)

Founded in 1916 as a chapter of the Grand Lodge of the State of New York, Independent Order of Odd Fellows. Members were Hungarian-speaking Jews who conducted their business in that language until 1939. Established a relief committee, a cemetery committee, loan fund, an old age and disability fund. Affiliated with the Pannonia Rebekah Lodge No. 130, I.O.O.F.

Minutes, of regular meetings, 1920-39 (Hungarian), 1939-42, 1952-63 (English); of the Burial Committee, 1920-36 (Hungarian); of the Old Age Pension and Disability Committee, 1934-42 (Hungarian), 1944-62 (English) of the Silver Jubilee Committee, 1940-41; financial records, 1921-37 (Hungarian), 1950's-70's (English); correspondence, Disability Committee, 1940's-50's; miscellaneous, including materials pertaining to the Pannonia Rebekah Lodge.

ILINTSY
Vinnitsa province,
Ukrainian SSR

73. Elinitzer Kranken Unterstitzungs Verein
Records, 1945-1976, 5" (RG 891)

Founded in 1895. At one time owned a synagogue on Clinton Street, New York. Maintained a loan fund for members.

Constitution; minutes, 1946-75; financial records, 1945-59; loan fund materials; correspondence pertaining to burial; membership records, 1930's-50's.

JANOW
Poland

74. Chaim Hersch Weiss First Janower Sick and Benevolent Association
Records, 1928-1972, 1' 5½" (RG 868)

Organized in 1909. A group of Stanislav *landslayt* joined c. 1910. Established loan and relief funds; a Passover fund for *landslayt*. Named after a rabbi from Janow, Poland. Dissolved 1973.

Constitutions; minutes, 1948-72; financial records, 1931-68; membership records; cemetery maps; correspondence; seal; stamps.

JEKABPILS, YEKABPILS
(Ger. Jakobstadt), Latvian SSR. Latvian Republic, 1918-1940

See Kreitzburger Jacobstadter Benevolent Association, entry 110.

JEZIORANY
(Yid. Yezierne)
Olsztyn province, Poland (formerly E. Prussia)

75. First Yezierna Sick and Benevolent Society
Records, 1900-1973, 1' 5½" (RG 950)

Founded in 1899 "to help the members in the event of sickness and distress." Also known as the First Jezierna Chevra. Dissolved in the 1970's.

Constitution; minutes, 1938-72; financial records, 1953-73; materials pertaining to burial; correspondence; miscellaneous; seal.

All dressed up for the ball. Phyllis Pearl (left) and Rosaline (née Dukalsky) Schwartz at the annual ball of the Independent Greidinger Sick and Benevolent Association. (Donated by Phyllis Pearl)

KALISZ
Lodz province, Poland

76. Kalisher Social Verein
Records, 1962-1977, 1" (RG 1049)

Founded in 1929. Worked with the Kalisher memorial book committee to publish a memorial book.

Constitution, 1962; minutes, 1972-77; bulletins.

KALUSH
(Pol. Kalusz)
Stanislav province,
Ukrainian SSR*

77. Kaluszer Ladies Society, Inc.
Records, 1958-1974, 1½" (RG 959)

Organized in 1919. Also known as the Kalisher (or Kalusher) Ladies Society, Inc. Dissolved 1974.

Minutes, 1958-74 (German); seal.

KAMENETS
(Pol. Kamieniec Litewski)
Brest province,
Belorussian SSR

78. Kamenetzer Litovsker Memorial Committee
Records, 1928-1970, 5" (RG 968)

Founded in 1961 to publish a memorial book and to coordinate annual memorial meetings of Kamenetzer societies. Affiliated organizations are: Kamenetz-Litovsker Women's Malbish Arumim (clothe the poor) League, Cong. Kochob Jacob Anshei Kamenetz, Lite, Ladies Auxiliary of the Kamenetzer Shul, Kamenetz-Litovsker Young Friends Workmen's Circle Branch 309, Lopates Family Circle, Rudnitzky Cousins Club, Bonchik Family Circle, Kamenetz Litovsker U.V.

Minutes, financial records, Women's Malbish Arumim League, 1950's-60's; correspondence; meeting notices; anniversary journals, of the Lopates F.C. and Kamenetz Litovsker U.V.; memorial book, 1970; publication materials pertaining to the memorial book.

KAMENETS-PODOLSKI
Ukrainian SSR

79. Kamenetz-Podoler Relief Organization
Records, 1945-1974, 2½" (RG 972)

Founded in 1944 to furnish "aid and assistance for the relief of human suffering in the city of Kamenetz Podolsk, U.S.S.R. and to the residents and former residents...who suffered from war, nazism and fascism..." Rehabilitated refugees; built children's village in Israel.

Certificate of incorporation, 1945; by-laws; anniversary journals; correspondence; meeting notices; photographs; memorial book, 1965.

See also Zinkowitzer and Kamenetz Podolier Society, entry 260.

KEDAINIAI
(Rus. Keidany)
Lithuanian SSR
Lithuanian Republic,
1918-1940

80. Keidaner Association
Records, 1930-1949, 1½" (RG 1048)

Established in 1900. Associated with the Keidaner Ladies Aid Society of the Keidaner Orphan Asylum. Sponsored loan, relief, Passover funds to aid needy *landslayt* in Kedainiai.

Anniversary journals, 1930, 1940; monthly bulletin of the association and the Keidaner Ladies Aid Society, 1936-49.

KHOTIN, HOTIN
Chernovtsy province,
Ukrainian SSR
Rumania, 1918-1940
(in Bessarabia)

81. Chotiner-Bessarabier Emergency Club
Records, 1971-1980, 1½" (RG 1052)

Established 1930 to provide emergency funds for needy members who could not pay rent, utility bills, etc. Provided no sick or death benefits or burial; members of the club received these benefits through membership in other societies.

Minutes, 1972-80; photograph.

KIELCE
Kielce province,
Poland

82. Kieltzer Sick and Benevolent Society of New York
Records, 1927-1980, 2½" (RG 1056)

Organized in 1905 as the Kieltzer Sick and Benevolent Society of Russian Poland, Inc. Maintained a loan fund for members; provided housing for new arrivals. Associated with a ladies auxiliary, founded 1923, for charitable activity. Affiliated with the Kieltzer and Chenchiner Relief to aid *landslayt*. Changed name in 1954 to present title.

Constitution; souvenir journals, 1927, 1980; of the Kieltzer and Chenchiner Relief Committee, 1937, 1941; publication by the Committee for the Resettlement of Kielcer Jews, 1946.

KIROVOGRAD
(formerly Yelizavetgrad)
Kirovograd province,
Ukrainian SSR

83. Independent Elizabethgrad Ladies Benevolent Association
Records, 1961-1975, 5" (RG 861)

Founded in 1905. This women's society owned its own cemetery plots. Activities included support for Israel. Dissolved 1975.

Financial records, 1960's-70's.

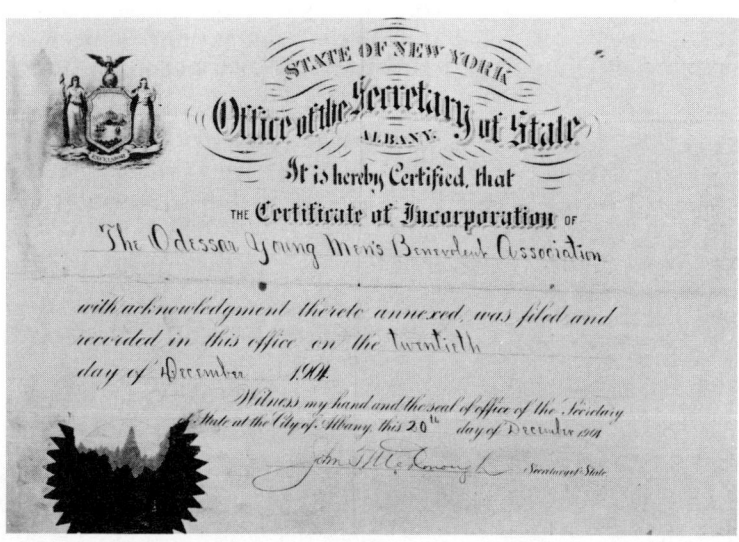

Incorporation certificate of the Odessar Young Men's Benevolent Association, 1901. (Donated by the Odessar Young Men's Benevolent Association)

KLEVAN
(Pol. Klewan)
Rovno province,
Ukrainian SSR*

84. First Klevaner Sick and Benevolent Society
Records, 1944-1973, 1'3" (RG 881)

Founded in 1902. Original purpose included establishment of a synagogue. Also known as the Klevaner-Voliner B.A. Activities included the establishment of a *gmiles-khesed* (free loan fund) for its impoverished members in the 1930's and relief work for *landslayt* in Klevan after WWI and WWII.

Constitution; minutes, 1944-66; financial records, 1940's-70's; correspondence, 1960's-70's; banner.

KLIMONTOW
Kielce province,
Poland

85. First Klimontover Sick Benevolent Society
Records, 1915-1921, 3" (RG 969)

Founded in 1905. Organized a relief committee in the 1940's to aid survivors. Assisted rabbi from the home town to come to New York and head a congregation.

Minutes, 1917-21; financial records, 1915-21.

KNIHININ
Stanislav province,
Ukrainian SSR*

86. Erster Knihinin Stanislauer K.U.V.
Records, 1937-1977, 7½" (RG 1090)

Organized in 1907 with twenty members. Maintained a loan fund. Dissolved 1977.

Minutes, 1953-68 (German, English); financial records, 1937-77; membership list, 1968; seal.

KOLBUSZOWA
Lwow province,
Poland

87. Kolbuszowa Relief Association, Inc.
Records, 1919-1967, 5½" (RG 888)

Organized after WWI by members of the Kolbuszower Young Men's Benevolent Society to aid inhabitants of Kolbuszowa. Was active in the 1930's; incorporated in 1942. Erected a monument to Holocaust victims; sent packages to *landslayt* in Poland and Israel. Affiliated organizations included: Kolbuszower Y.M.B.S., Kolbuszower Chevrah Bnei Chaim Machnei Reuben, Kolbushover Teitelbaum Wallach Lodge No. 98, Ind. Order Brith Abraham.

Certificate of incorporation, 1942; constitution; minutes, 1946-48; financial records, 1940's, 60's; publications and journals, 1930's-40's; materials from Kolbuszowa; photographs; memorial book, 1971; materials of the Kolbuszower Teitelbaum Ferbriderungs Ferayn Cong., 1913; Kolbushover Teitelbaum Wallach Lodge No. 98, I.O.B.A.

88. Kolbuszower Young Men's Benevolent Society
Records, 1919-1974, 5" (RG 957)

Organized in 1899. Members organized the Kolbuszowa Relief Association after WWI. Aided Kolbuszowa; Jewish charities in America.

Constitution; minutes, 1953-74; anniversary journals, 1919-49.

KOLO
Lodz province,
Poland

89. Chevra Ahavath Achim B'nai Kolo, Inc.
Records, 1918, 1940-1979, 1½" (RG 1057)

Established in 1877 to maintain a synagogue, originally located at 48 Avenue D, New York, to help the needy in Kolo. Cooperated with the Kolo *landsmanshaft* in Israel to aid survivors there and publish a memorial book.

Constitutions; memorial meeting minutes, 1975; financial records; souvenir journals, 1940, 1978; correspondence; bulletins, 1946-79; memorial book, 1958; miscellaneous.

KOLOMYYA
Stanislav province,
Ukrainian SSR*

90. Kolomear Friends Association
Records, 1906-1973, 1'8" (RG 792)

Originally organized in 1904 for the purpose of founding a synagogue. Also called Tsvishn (among) Kolomear Young Friends. Formed the United Kolomear Relief during WWI and the Refugee Committee during WWII.

Constitutions; minutes, 1939-54; financial documents, 1953-72; membership ledger; application forms, 1907-56; membership books pertaining to illness, sick and death benefits, 1933-67; journal, 1929; memorial book, 1957; photographs.

KONSKIE
(Yid. Kinsk, Rus. Konsk)
Kielce province,
Poland

91. Independent Kinsker Aid Association
Records, 1930-1980, 5" (RG 911)

Founded in 1904. Maintained a relief committee after WWII to aid survivors who came to the U.S. Sent food packages to *landslayt* in Israel.

Financial records, 1930's-50's; correspondence; journal; miscellaneous.

KOPISTY
Czechoslovakia

92. Kopister Benevolent Association
Records, 1951-1976, 2½" (RG 943)

Organized in 1905. Benefits included wedding and *shive* (seven-day mourning period) funds. Also held lectures. Aided home town in early years. Dissolved 1976.

Minutes, 1951-76; financial records.

KOPRZYWNICA
(Yid. Pokshivnitsa)
Kielce province,
Poland

93. Pokshivnitzer Relief Committee
Records, 1934-1971, 12½" (RG 908)

Founded c. 1930's for purposes of overseas relief. Burial plots were secured through an affiliated group, the Chevra Divrei Chaim. Close relations have been maintained with the Pokshivnitzer *landsmanshaftn* in Israel.

Minutes, 1944-58; financial records; correspondence, including with Pokshivnitzer society in Israel; with Chevra Divrei Chaim; photographs; miscellaneous.

KOPYCHINTSY
(Pol. Kopyczynce)
Ternopol province,
Ukrainian SSR*

94. First Kopyczynzer Sick and Benevolent Society
Records, 1943-1975, 2½" (RG 970)

Founded in 1895. Also known as the Erste Kopyczyncer K.U.V. Dissolved in the 1970's.

Cemetery records; correspondence; seal.

KOPYL
Bobruisk province,
Belorussian SSR

95. Kipiler Young Men's Benevolent Association
Records, 1958-1972, 2½" (RG 1044)

Organized in 1925. Supported institutions in the home town. Provided free loans for members.

Minutes, 1958-72; banner.

KOROPETS
(Pol. Koropiec)
Ternopol province,
Ukrainian SSR*

96. First Koropiecer Benevolent Association
Records, 1967-1975, 2½" (RG 946)

Organized in 1909. Numbered 83 members in 1938. Dissolved 1976.

Financial records; seal.

KOROSTYSHEV
Zhitomir province,
Ukrainian SSR

97. Korostishever Aid Society
Records, 1920-1953, 2½" (RG 791)

Founded in Detroit, Michigan, in 1920 after a conference held there to unite American Korostishever *landslayt* to aid their home town. Affiliated with the Relief Committee for War and Pogrom Sufferers of Korostishev (United Korostitchev Relief). Established a ladies auxiliary, c. 1930.

Anniversary journal, 1950, including membership directories for New York, Chicago, Detroit, Los Angeles *landsmanshaftn*; miscellaneous.

Passport photograph of relief delegate (sheliekh) Harry Nachimoff and his scrupulously kept account of cash disbursements made to individuals and organizations in Wolkowisk donated by family members and the Wolkowisk society in New York. (Donated by the Wolkowisker Relief Society)

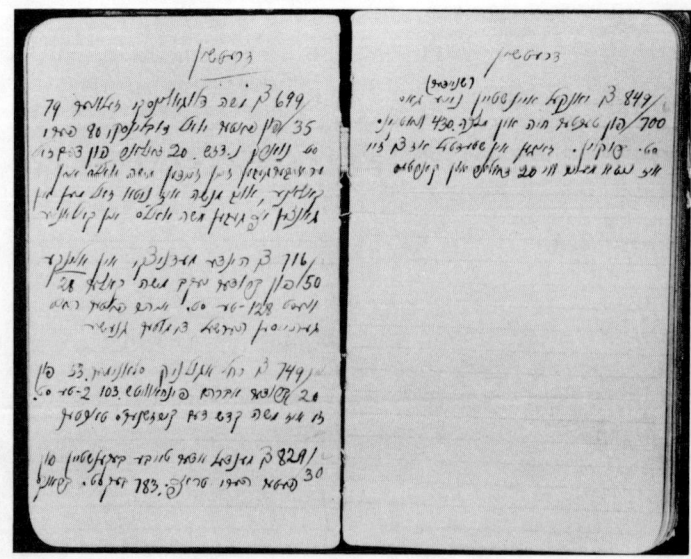

KORSUN
Kiev province,
Ukrainian SSR

98. Chevra Ahavas Achim Anshei Korson, Kiev province
Records, 1923-1946, 5" (RG 418)

Organized in 1894. Established a synagogue; supported charitable institutions in Korsun and the U.S. Met at 98 Forsyth Street, New York.

Pinkes (record book), containing minutes and membership lists, 1923-46.

See also Horodishter Korsoner Lodge, Inc., entry 64.

KOSICE
Kosice province,
Slovakia, Czechoslovakia

99. Kosice and Vicinity Chapter 59, Bnai Zion
Records, 1966-1978, 1" (RG 790)

Founded in 1952 for philanthropic purposes and to locate survivors from Kosice. Affiliate of the Zionist fraternal organization, Bnai Zion.

Correspondence, 1976-78; bulletins, invitations, 1966-77; personal materials of donor; photographs.

KOVEL
Volyn province,
Ukrainian SSR*

100. Progressive Kovler Young Friends Branch 475, Workmen's Circle
Records, 1908-1948, 10" (RG 866)

Founded in 1908 and affiliated with the Workmen's Circle, 1910. Established a relief committee during WWI; dispatched a delegate to Kovel to distribute aid to *landslayt*. After WWII, provided aid to Israel together with other Kovler organizations.

Minutes, regular and executive meetings, 1917-48; membership records, 1908-10; miscellaneous, including materials pertaining to the Workmen's Circle, 1917-22.

KRAKES
(Yid. Krok)
Kaunas (Kovno) province,
Lithuanian SSR,
Lithuanian Republic,
1918-1940

101. Kroker Benevolent Association
Records, 1899, 1910-1977, 5" (RG 789)

Founded in 1908. Formed a separate relief committee during WWI.

Minutes, 1910, 1916, 1938; financial records; membership records; chart of members' cemetery plots, 1931-68; announcements, speeches, invitations, some in rhyme form, 1910-77; photographs; miscellaneous documents from Krok and the U.S.

KRASNIK
Lublin province,
Poland

102. Congregation Anshei Krashnik
Records, 1905-1976, 5" (RG 815)

Founded in 1897. Established a relief committee after WWI. Sent financial assistance to Krashnik *landsmanshaft* in Israel.

Minutes, 1929-72; financial records, including cemetery deeds, 1906-54; jubilee journals; memorial book, 1973; miscellaneous, including materials pertaining to society in Israel.

KRASNOBROD
Lublin province,
Poland

103. First Krasnobroder Aid Society
Records, 1922-1934, 1″ (RG 1012)

Founded and incorporated in 1912. Established a *moes-khitim* (Passover fund) committee to aid *landslayt* in home town; a *gmiles-khesed* (free loan fund) to aid members in New York.

Minutes, 1922-29; materials pertaining to society's secretary's political activities in Krasnobrod, 1929-34; photographs.

KRASNYSTAW
Lublin province,
Poland

104. First Krasnystauer Young Men's Benevolent Society
Records, 1940-1955, 2½″ (RG 1051)

Founded in 1915. Maintained an emergency fund for members in need. Conducted extensive relief during WWII.

Constitution; minutes, 1940-54.

KREMENCHUG
Poltava province,
Ukrainian SSR

105. Krementchuger Ladies Benevolent Association
Records, 1914, 1939-1977, 10″ (RG 1087)

Established in 1900 and incorporated in 1914 as the Ladies Krementshuger Benevolent Association (also known as the First Ladies Krementshuger B.A.). Provided burial; supported philanthropic institutions.

Certificate of incorporation, 1914; minutes, 1960-76; financial records, 1940's-70's; membership directory; correspondence; cemetery map; miscellaneous.

KREMENETS
(Pol. Krzemieniec)
Ternopol province,
Ukrainian SSR*

106. Kremenitzer Wolyner Benevolent Association
Records, 1935-1977, 8″ (RG 788)

Founded in 1915. Formed a relief committee during WWI. Built a library in Israel after WWII.

Constitution; minutes, 1967-74; financial records, 1946-58; correspondence; anniversary journals; periodical published by Kremenitzer in Israel; memorial books, 1954, 1965.

KRIVICHI
(Pol. Krzywicze)
Molodechno province,
Belorussian SSR*

107. Erster Krzywcza An San Benevolent Society
Records, 1908, 1946-1966, 1″ (RG 1013)

Founded in 1920. Established a relief committee after WWI to aid institutions in home town. Affiliated with a Krzywczer society in Israel that provides relief for indigent members.

Minutes, 1946-66; *ksube* (marriage contract) of society secretary, 1908.

108. Young Krevitzer
Records, 1958, 1964-1976, 2½″ (RG 954)

Founded c. 1901. Dissolved 1976.

Minutes; materials pertaining to dues, finances, sick benefits, burial; seal.

KRIVOYE OZERO
Odessa province,
Ukrainian SSR*

109. Krivozer Fraternal Society of Greater New York
Records, 1927-1961, 5" (RG 912)

Formed in 1918 to send a *landsman* to California for a tuberculosis treatment; later developed to provide mutual aid for members. Between WWI and II conducted extensive relief and refugee relocation work as well as support of a farm established by Krivozer Jews on land alloted by the Soviet government. Recent activities include aid to Israel. Affiliated groups were: Krivozer Beneficial Association of Philadelphia, Independent Krivozer Ladies Auxiliary (est'd. 1927), committees in Chicago, Boston, Lawrence, Mass., St. Paul, Minn., Canada.

Minutes, 1933-47; financial records, 1950's-60's; anniversary journal; miscellaneous.

KRUSTPILS
(Ger. Kreuzberg)
Latvian SSR,
Latvian Republic,
1918-1940

110. Kreitzburger Jacobstadter Benevolent Association
Records, 1921-1977, 7½" (RG 944)

Founded in 1918 with 100 members. Dissolved 1977.

Minutes, 1942-76; financial records, 1951-77; membership records; sick benefit and cemetery materials; correspondence.

Subscription fund flyer to aid the political prisoners of Smela who were interned in Siberia. (Donated by the Cherkasser-Smela Benevolent Association, Inc.)

Receipt from the Relief Committee for the Smieler Political Convicts who were interned in Siberia, July 1913. (Donated by the Cherkasser-Smela Benevolent Association, Inc.)

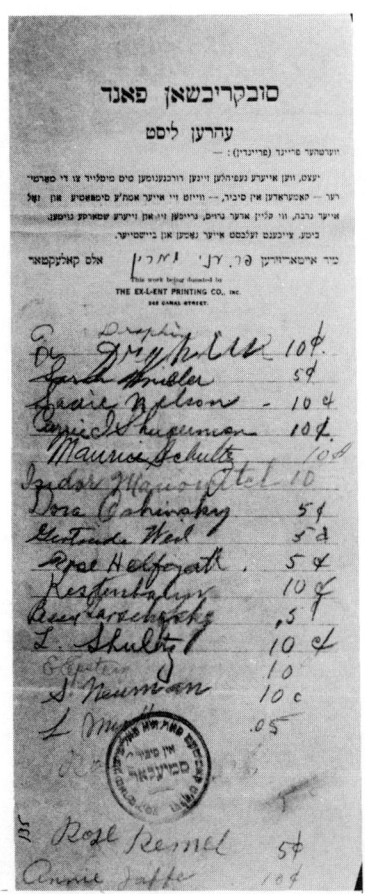

KRYSTYNOPOL
Lvov province,
Ukrainian SSR*

111. First Krystonopoler Sick and Benevolent Society
Records, 1947-1974, 2½" (RG 971)

Founded in 1895. Originally owned a synagogue. In early years sent *moes-khitim* (Passover funds) to *landslayt* in home town; continue practice currently with recent Russian immigrants to U.S. Organized a relief committee between WWI and II.

Constitution; financial records, 1947-59.

KUDRYNCE
Ternopol province,
Ukrainian SSR*

112. Kudryncer Benevolent Society, Inc.
Records, 1940-1978, 7½" (RG 787)

Organized in 1900 as the Independent First Kudryncer Congregation Sick and Aid Society. Maintained a loan fund; synagogue on Houston Street, New York.

Constitution; minutes, 1943-69; souvenir journal, 1955; correspondence, 1978; newspaper clippings; wooden ballot box.

KULACZKOWCE
Stanislav province,
Ukrainian SSR*

113. First Kulaczkowitzer Kranken Untershtitsung Verein
Records, 1913-1952, 1965, 7½" (RG 783)

Organized in 1911; chartered in 1913. Associated with a ladies auxiliary.

Minutes, 1913-55; financial records, 1928-46; funeral parlor receipt books, 1913-52, 1965.

KUPIN
Kamenets-Podolski province,
Ukrainian SSR

114. Kupiner-Podolier Memorial Committee
Records, 1939-1979, 1" (RG 1058)

Since 1960 has held annual memorial meetings for Kupiner *landslayt* killed in WWII. *Landslayt* belonging to various Kupiner societies participate.

Minutes, 1960-77; of the Monish Kupersmith Kupiner Circle, 1939-47; of the Kupiner Podolier Br. 329 Workmen's Circle, 1945; short history of Kupin.

KUTNO
Lodz province,
Poland

115. Kutno Society Bnai Jacob
Records, 1884-1974, 10" (RG 857)

Organized in 1872. Activities included support of Hebrew Immigrant Aid Society (HIAS) and Israel. Dissolved 1974.

Minutes, 1953-74; financial records, 1946-74; burial permits, 1884-1974; miscellaneous; cemetery map; seals.

KUTY
Stanislav province,
Ukrainian SSR*

116. Ray Heit Chapter of the Kittever Ladies Relief Auxiliary
Records, 1947-1975, 1979-1980, 5" (RG 985)

Established in 1947 as the Kittever Ladies Relief Auxiliary. Worked with the Kittever Sick and Benevolent Society to provide aid for surviving *landslayt* after WWII. Renamed for Ray Heit, the first auxiliary president. Disbanded 1980.

Minutes, 1947-80; financial records, 1948-60; meeting announcements; photographs; memorial book, 1958.

LESZNIOW
Ternopol province,
Ukrainian SSR*

117. First Lesznower Sick and Benevolent Society Sons of Jacob Solomon
Records, 1910-1977, 5" (RG 926)

Established in 1903. Originally was a religious society which rented a loft on the Lower East Side where members could pray on weekends.

Minutes, 1964-75; financial records, 1962-77; records pertaining to sick benefits and burial; membership list; correspondence; seal.

LETICHEV
Kamenets-Podolski province,
Ukrainian SSR

118. Latichever Progressive Society, Inc.
Records, 1939-1975, 7½" (RG 897)

Incorporated in 1924. Acquired title to cemetery lot in Montefiore Cemetery from the surviving trustees of the First Latichever Lodge No. 224, Independent Order Brith Sholom, 1926. Maintained a loan fund. Dissolved 1979.

Financial records, 1950's-70's; membership lists; correspondence, 1939-76; materials pertaining to burial; miscellaneous.

LIPKANY
Moldavian SSR
(in Bessarabia)

See Grodner-Lipkaner Branch 74, Workmen's Circle, entry 65.

LODZ
Poland

119. Lodzer Young Ladies Aid Society
Records, 1954-1975, 2½" (RG 1095)

Founded in 1919 at a wedding reception of a member of their brother society, the Lodzer Young Men's Benevolent Society. Supported charities and Lodzer relief activities. Dissolved 1975.

Minutes, 1954-72; souvenir journal; meeting announcements.

120. Lodzer Young Men's Benevolent Society
Records, 1927-1943, 7½" (RG 1045)

Founded in 1902. Affiliated in 1915 with the General Relief Committee for Jewish War Sufferers in Lodz. Sent two delegates to Lodz in 1920 to bring relief funds; affiliated in 1935 with the United Emergency Committee for the City of Lodz. Associated with a ladies auxiliary, Lodzer Young Ladies Aid Society.

Anniversary journals, 1927-77; memorial book, 1943; correspondence, 1930's; newspaper clippings.

121. Associated Lodzer Ladies Aid Society, Inc.
Records, 1937-1973, 7½" (RG 966)

Founded in 1929 with 25 members. Paid funeral expenses; members received burial through their husbands' membership in other Lodzer societies. Affiliated with the United Lodzer Relief Committee (est'd. 1914).

Minutes, 1937-73; financial report, 1948; photograph; correspondence; minutes, United Lodzer Relief Comittee, 1961-67; miscellaneous Relief materials; materials of the United Emergency Committee for the City of Lodz.

LOGISHIN
(Pol. Lahiszyn)
Pinsk province,
Belorussian SSR*

122. Lahishiner Ladies Auxiliary
Records, 1942-1980, 5" (RG 896)

Founded in 1935 for social and charitable purposes by thirteen women at a meeting of the Lahishin Social Benevolent Society, the brother group. Since 1945 supported a child in a children's home in Israel. Dissolved 1980.

Minutes, 1965-77; financial records, 1950's-70's; materials pertaining to relief and charitable work; meeting announcements; 1948-80; gavels; stamp; materials of the Lahishin S.B.S.

LOMAZY
Lublin province,
Poland

123. Lomazer Young Men's and Women's Benevolent Association, Inc.
Records, 1956-1976, 2" (RG 817)

Founded in 1916. Active in relief work after WWI. including sending a delegate to Lomazy and providing funds to rebuild the synagogue, destroyed by fire. Relief work after WWII included sending funds and material assistance to *landslayt* in Displaced Persons Camps.

Constitution; jubilee journals, 1956, 1961, 1971, 1976.

The Associated Lodzer Ladies celebrate the golden wedding anniversary of member and husband, seated front center, c. 1936. (Donated by the Lodzer Young Men's Benevolent Society)

LOMZA
Bialystok province,
Poland

124. Lomzer Aid Society
Records, 1914-1917, 13" (RG 851)

Established in 1898 to help needy *landslayt*. In 1937 joined with four Lomzer organizations to form the United Lomzer Relief Committee to aid the town of Lomza. Sponsored a loan fund, mutual dues fund, *moes-khitim* (Passover funds).

Minutes, 1914-1939; financial reports, 1957-66; meeting announcements; "The Lomzer Bulletin," 1946-56; materials relating to anniversary celebrations; materials pertaining to publication of Lomzer memorial book; golden book (record of deaths of members) of the *khevre-kedishe* (burial committee) of the Lomzer Aid Society; materials pertaining to other Lomzer organizations: Lomzer Shul – Anshe Lomza V'Gatch, Lomzer Ladies Relief Society, United Lomzer Relief Committee; miscellaneous.

LOPUSZNA
USSR

125. First Independent Loposhner Society, Inc.
Records, 1930, 5" (RG 876)

Organized in 1915. Activities included establishment of a free loan fund for its members.

Constitution; membership record book, an oversize bound volume presented to the society by the Dzuriker Sick Benevolent Association, 1930; grave reservation receipts.

LUBAN
Poland

126. Lubaner and Vicinity Benevolent Society
Records, 1941-1976, 7½" (RG 945)

Founded in 1923. Supported Jewish causes and charitable organizations. Dissolved in the 1970's.

Minutes, 1965-76; financial records, 1964-76; cemetery records; correspondence; meeting notices; dissolution ballots.

LUTOWISKA
Lvov province,
Ukrainian SSR*

127. Lutowisker Young Men's Benevolent Society
Records, 1922-1978, 1'8" (RG 827)

Founded in 1911. Established a loan fund for its members. Activities included sending relief to *landslayt* in Israel after WWII.

Constitutions; minutes, 1922-48, 1953-72; financial records, 1941-65, 1978; membership applications, 1936-65, and other records; sick benefit applications, 1930-58; anniversary journals; cemetery maps; gavel; stamp; banner.

LUTSK
(Pol. Luck)
Volyn province,
Ukrainian SSR*

128. Independent Lutzker Aid Society
Records, 1914-1976, 12½" (RG 904)

Founded in Brooklyn in 1914 and incorporated that same year. Associated with the Ladies Auxiliary, established 1927. Affiliated with the United Lutzker Relief Committee.

Certificate of incorporation, 1914; constitution; minutes, 1935-40, 1961-76; financial records, 1915-66; books of the Old Age Fund; anniversary journals; materials pertaining to other New York Lutsker societies: First Lutzker Benevolent Association, United Lutzker Y.M.&Y.L.A., Lutzker Br. 538, Workmen's Circle, United Lutzker Relief Committee; miscellaneous; banners, Ind. Lutzker Aid Society, Ladies Auxiliary of the I.L.A.S.

LYAKHOVICHI
(Pol. Lachowicze)
Baranovichi province,
Belorussian SSR*

129. Lechowitzer Ladies Auxiliary
Records, 1946-1961, 3" (RG 990)

Founded in 1934 to raise funds to support home town and New York charities; provide social functions. Affiliated with the Congregation Bnai Isaac Anshei Lechowitz, established 1889. Met in the congregation's building at 217 Henry Street, New York.

Minutes, 1952-60; financial records, 1947-56; meeting announcements, including notices of the Cong. Anshei Lechowitz.

LYUBAR
(Yid. Luber)
Zhitomir province,
Ukrainian SSR

130. First Luberer Benevolent Association
Records, 1937-1976, 2½" (RG 998)

Established in 1895. Provided loan funds for members without interest. After WWII maintained a Luberer Relief Organization together with other *landsmanshaftn* to aid survivors in Israel and South America.

Constitution; minutes, 1969-76; financial reports; anniversary journals.

MAKOW,
MAKOW MAZOWIECKI
Warszawa province,
Poland

131. Makover Unterstitzungs Verein
Records, 1952-1976, 5" (RG 942)

Founded c. 1925. Dissolved 1976.

Minutes, 1952-76; financial records, 1952-77; materials pertaining to burial.

132. Makower Young Men's Aid Society
Records, 1915-1969, 3" (RG 1043)

Founded in 1907. Affiliated with the United Makower Relief established after WWI to aid *landslayt* and reestablished in 1945 to aid war survivors.

Correspondence; photographs (64) from Makow, 1915-1940's; memorial book, 1969.

MIDDLE VILLAGE
Queens, New York

133. Middle Village Benevolent Association, Inc.
Records, 1962-1974, 5" (RG 988)

Established in 1925. Met in Congregation Machziki Harav, Queens. Dissolved 1975.

Financial records, 1971-75; materials pertaining to burial, 1962-74; seal.

MIEDZYRZEC, MIEDZYRZEC PODLASKI
(Yid. Meserits)
Lublin province, Poland

134. Independent Meseritzer Young Men's Association
Records, 1911-1977, 10" (RG 823)

Founded in 1901. Activities included the formation of a relief committee after WWI and sending delegates to the home town where the society established an orphanage, a loan society, a hospital. Instrumental in founding the United Meseritzer Relief, Inc., 1936, through which it aided *landslayt* before WWII and after the war in Israel.

Constitution; minutes, 1911-37, 1949-68; newsletter; memorial book, 1978; miscellaneous.

135. United Meseritzer Relief, Inc.
Records, 1952-1957, 2½" (RG 822)

Established in 1936 as a committee of delegates from eight Meseritzer *landsmanshaftn* to provide relief to *landslayt* in the home town, Europe, and new areas of settlement. Aided war survivors; brought a group of Meseritzer orphans to a farm in Canada; established a free loan fund, bristle cooperative, apartment complex, center for *landslayt* in Israel.

Minutes, regular and executive meetings, 1952-57; miscellaneous, including speeches, appeals.

Members of the Federation of Bessarabian Societies of America prepare relief packages for their home town in Russia during WWII, New York, 1941. (Donated by Rose Schwartz)

MIKHAILOVKA
(until 1946, Mikhalpol)
Kamenets-Podolski
province, Ukrainian SSR

136. Michalpolier Podolier Benevolent Association
Records, 1925-1967, 2½″ (RG 1009)

Established in 1925. Worked with a ladies auxiliary. Contributed to Jewish philanthropies.

Minutes, 1925-67.

MIKULINTSY
(Pol. Mikulince)
Ternopol province,
Ukrainian SSR*

137. Mikulincer Independent Lodge, Inc.
Records, 1961-1974, 5″ (RG 948)

Founding date unknown. Provided *shive* (seven days of mourning) benefits for members. Active until 1975.

Financial records, 1960's-70's.

138. First Independent Mikulincer Sick and Benevolent Association
Records, 1910-1956, 1′3½″ (RG 828)

Founded in 1899. Was joined by the First Mikulinzer Lodge No. 556, Independent Order Brith Abraham (est'd. 1909); they apparently merged in the 1940's.

Minutes, 1918-50's (German, Yiddish); of the First Mikulinzer Lodge, 1910-28 (German); record book of the burial committee, 1920's; financial records, 1940's-50's, including membership dues book, 1924-31; correspondence; miscellaneous.

MINSK
Minsk province,
Belorussian SSR

139. Minsker Ladies Benevolent Society
Records, 1948, 1957-1974, 5″ (RG 907)

Organized in 1895. Provided sick and death benefits, burial for its members. Dissolved 1974.

Minutes, 1970-71; financial records, 1957-70; materials pertaining to burial; correspondence.

MOGIELNICA
(Rus. Mogelnitse)
Warszawa province,
Poland

140. Independent Mogelnitzer Benevolent Society
Records, 1910-1929, 1945, 3″ (RG 984)

Organized in 1906. Maintained a relief committee. Affiliated with an organization of Mogelnitzer in Israel; supported a loan fund there.

Minutes, 1910-29; materials pertaining to relief drives.

MOGILEV, MOHILEV
Mogilev province,
Belorussian SSR,
on Dnieper River

141. Congregation Ahavath Achim Anshei Mohilev on Dnieper
Records, 1913, 1961-1974, 1½" (RG 1061)

Incorporated in 1913 as Congregation Ahavath Achim Anshe Mohilev al Nahar Dnieper, a religious corporation. Dissolved in the 1970's.

Certificate of incorporation, 1913; financial materials; burial permits; correspondence.

MYSZYNIEC
(Yid. Mishnits),
Bialystok province,
Poland

142. Progressive Mishnitzer Young Men's Society
Records, 1936, 1948-1975, 5" (RG 913)

Founded in 1911. Provided members with cultural events such as lectures on labor questions. Supported institutions in Mishnits.

Minutes, 1948-75; anniversary journal; photograph.

NAREW
Bialystok province,
Poland

143. Narevker Untershtitsungs Verein
Records, 1960-1974, 5" (RG 1092)

Organized in 1890 with 13 members. Associated with a ladies auxiliary.

Minutes, 1968-74; financial records, including sick benefits payment book, 1940's-50's; records of the Narevker Ladies Auxiliary, 1960-73; miscellaneous; stamp.

NASIELSK
(Yid. Nashelsk)
Warszawa province,
Poland

144. United Nashelsker Relief Society of Los Angeles
Records, 1955-1978, 2½" (RG 976)

Organized in 1945; adopted constitution, 1957. Main objective to aid Nashelsker *landslayt* in Israel. Also known as the Nashelsker Society of Los Angeles. Built housing settlement, community center, synagogue, library, nursery, air raid shelter in Israel. Had affiliated youth group named the Scions.

Constitution; minutes; financial records; anniversary journals; convention bulletins; speeches.

NEMIROV
Lvov province,
Ukrainian SSR*

145. Independent Nemirover Benevolent Society, Inc.
Records, 1964-1975, 5" (RG 933)

Founded in 1905; incorporated 1906. Dissolved 1975.

Minutes, 1964-75; financial records; membership records; correspondence; seal.

NEW YORK
New York

146. The New York Social Club
Records, 1953-1954, 7½" (RG 955)

Organized in 1883 and incorporated in 1885 for benevolent, literary, dramatic, and musical purposes. Met in Chelsea Hall, New York in the 1960's.

Certificate of incorporation, 1885; financial records; miscellaneous; gavels; seal; pennant.

147. Independent Greater New York Sick and Benevolent Association
Records, 1915-1947, 1½″ (RG 1060)

Established in 1897 by garment workers as a fraternal organization not limited to *landslayt*. Maintained loan and old age funds; its own burial committee which prepared the bodies of its members for burial. Later merged with lodges in the Knights of Pythias.

Constitution; minutes, 1947; souvenir journals, 1927-47; armband of burial committee.

NIEMENCZYN
(Yid. Nemenzin),
Wilno province,
Belorussian SSR*

148. Nemenziner Benevolent Association
Records, 1958-1976, 5″ (RG 941)

Founding date unknown. Dissolved 1976.

Minutes, 1958-76; financial records, 1960's-70's.

NIKOLAYEV
Nikolayev province,
Ukrainian SSR

149. Nickolayever Unterstitzungs Verein of Chicago
Records, 1939-1970, 3″ (RG 1063)

Organized in Chicago, 1927. Conducted relief drives during WWI, WWII. Worked with the Ladies Auxiliary of the Nickolayever U.V. in charitable work.

Souvenir journals, 1938-54; bulletins; miscellaneous.

NOVOSELITSA
Chernovtsy province,
Ukrainian SSR

150. United Novoselitzer Relief, Inc.
Records, 1945-1949, 5″ (RG 999)

Founding date unknown. Aided surviving *landslayt* after WWII by sending them funds, relief parcels, packages. Contributing organizations included: First Novoselitzer S.B.S., Independent Novoselitzer Ladies Verband, Novoselitzer-Bessarabian Prog. Workmen's Circle Br. 498, Independent Novoselitzer Bessarabian K.U.V., Bukawinaer Society.

Financial records, 1945-49; materials pertaining to relief work, including card files and account sheets of relief recipients and their addresses.

NOVYE STRELISHCHE
(Pol. Strzeliska Nowe)
Drogobych province,
Ukrainian SSR*

151. Strelisker Young Men's Benevolent Association
Records, 1934-1953, 2½″ (RG 1035)

Organized in 1905. Established an endowment fund in 1947 for members.

Minutes, 1934-53; journal, 1935.

NOWY KORCZYN
(Yid. Nayshtut)
Kielce province,
Poland

152. United Neustadter-Epstein Society of New York
Records, 1930's, 1956-1973, 2½" (RG 1011)

Formed in 1962 by a merger of the Neustadter Progressive Y.M.B.A. (est'd. 1911) with the Epstein Unterstitsungs Verein (est'd. 1904); named after a famous rabbi of Neustadt. The two societies supported the talmud-torah (free religious school) in the town; sent *moes-khitim* (Passover funds) to needy *landslayt*.

Minutes, of the Neustadter Prog. Y.M.B.A., 1956-62; of the merged society, through 1973; meeting announcements; photographs.

NOWY SACZ
(Yid. Sandz)
Krakow province,
Poland

153. Sandzer Society, Inc.
Records, 1943-1971, 5" (RG 922)

Founded in 1940 with the aim of aiding the unfortunate in Sandz. The eminent Jewish historian, Raphael Mahler, was affiliated with the society and edited their memorial book, *Sefer Sanz*.

Constitution; membership list; souvenir journals; correspondence, much pertaining to memorial book publication; memorial book, 1970.

ODESSA
Ukrainian SSR

154. Odessa Young Men of Harlem Sick Benevolent Association
Records, 1898-1974, 5" (RG 975)

Established in 1912. Soon after, founded a ladies auxiliary which existed until 1925. Held joint functions with the "downtown" Odessa society. Organized the Odessa Home for the Aged. Dissolved 1973.

Certificate of incorporation, 1912; constitutions; minutes; financial records, 1952-70; materials pertaining to burial; anniversary journals; photograph; personal documents of Samuel Dix, charter member; banner.

155. Odessar Young Men's Benevolent Association
Records, 1950's-1968, 10" (RG 858)

Incorporated in 1901. Established a loan fund for members; paid dues to the Odessa Center League; supported Israel. Dissolved 1968.

Certificate of incorporation, 1901; minutes, 1961-67; financial records, 1950's-60's; burial permits, 1958-68; seal; stamps.

156. First Independent Odesser Ladies Sick Benevolent Association
Records, 1961-1972, 5" (RG 859)

Founding date unknown. Contributed to the Odessa Center League; supported Israel. Dissolved 1972.

Minutes, 1964-72; financial records, 1961-72.

OPOLE
Lublin province, Poland

157. Independent Opoler Benevolent Society
Records, 1929, 1941-1961, 2½" (RG 1032)

Founded in 1912; an Opoler Young Men's Society had been founded in 1906 and failed. Worked with a ladies auxiliary.

Membership records, 1941-61; anniversary journal, 1929; meeting announcements of the Independent Opoler Ladies Auxiliary; memorial book, 1977.

ORLA
Grodno province, Belorussian SSR*

158. Independent Orler Benevolent Society, Inc.
Records, 1890's-1957, 3" (RG 1023)

Founded in 1892 as a lodge affiliated with the Order Brith Abraham; became independent in 1919. Was affiliated with a sisterhood. In 1970, sued the Polish government for using the old Orler synagogue as a warehouse, winning the case.

Constitutions; golden book (record of deaths of members), including minutes of the *khevre-kedishe* (burial committee), 1890's-1957; anniversary journal; cemetery deed; photograph.

A certificate given by Jewish communal institutions in Ostre, Ukraine, to Baruch Mordecai Rabinovich upon his departure to America, 1930, attesting to his worthiness as a representative of Ostre Jews and asking for support from the Ostre landsmanshaft in New York. (Donated by Hersh Rabinovitch)

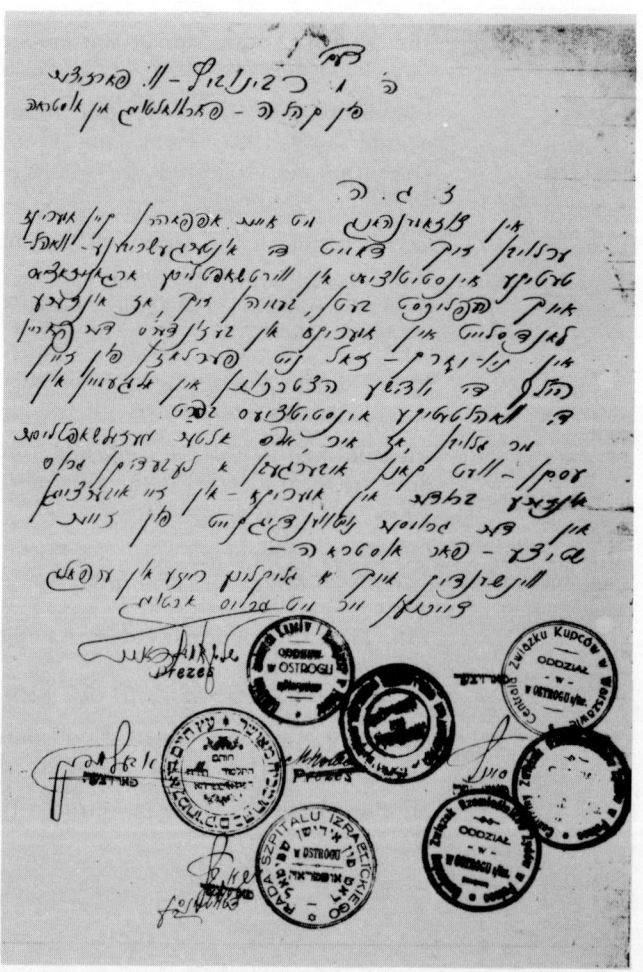

OSTROG
(Yid. Ostre)
Rovno province,
Ukrainian SSR*

159. Rabinovitch, Hersh (1896-1980)
Papers, 1930-1939, 1960's, 3" (RG 1071)

Papers reflect the communal activities of H. Rabinovitch's father, Baruch Mordecai Rabinovitch, born in Ostre-Volin, 1866; died in New York, 1939. Community officials in Ostre appointed him representative to the New York Ostre *landsmanshaft* upon his departure for the U.S., 1930.

Handwritten certificates honoring B.M.R.'s work on behalf of communal institutions in Ostre, 1930 (Hebrew); handwritten certificate (Yiddish) appointing B.M.R. as representative of community to N.Y. *landsmanshaft*; photographs; correspondence of Hersh Rabinovitch; memorial book of great rabbis and scholars, Ostre, 1907.

OSTROLEKA
(Rus. Ostrolenka)
Warszawa province,
Poland

160. Ostrolenker Friendship Society, Inc.
Records, 1918-1973, 10" (RG 860)

Organized as the Ostrolenker Lodge No. 607, Independent Order Brith Abraham, 1911. Filed for the incorporation of the Ostrolenker Friendship Society in 1950 and transferred cemetery property to the new membership corporation. Contributed to the Al Tidom Ass'n. (to aid Soviet Jews); the U.S. Grand Lodge of the I.O.B.A. Dissolved 1973; funds were disbursed to various Jewish charities.

Financial records, of the Ostrolenker Lodge, 1945-72; of the Friendship Society, 1950-73; correspondence, 1950's-60's, including correspondence pertaining to the Lodge; burial permits, Ostrolenker Lodge; seal, Ostrolenker Friendship Society.

161. Ostrolenker Progressive Young Friends
Records, 1920's, 1937-1970, 2½" (RG 1040)

Founded in 1912 by a group of *landslayt* who felt a need to belong to their own society, and not to the Independent Ostrolenker Young Men founded earlier. Joined the Ostrolenker Relief during WWI. Society's ladies auxiliary established 1932.

Constitution; minutes, 1939-70; journal, 1937; membership directory; photograph.

OTYNYA
(Pol. Ottynia)
Stanislav province,
Ukrainian SSR*

162. First Ottynier Young Men's Benevolent Association
Records, 1946-1967, 1970's, 5" (RG 1036)

Founded in 1900. Organized the United Ottynier Relief in 1914 which was active until 1950. Incorporated members of the Ottynier Young Ladies and Young Men's Progressive Ass'n. into the society in 1929. First Ottynier Ladies Aid Society organized in 1939.

Minutes, 1946-67; correspondence; bulletins, including short history of the society.

OZAROW
Kielce province,
Poland

163. Ozarower Young Men's Society
    Records, 1927-1977, 3" (RG 903)

Founded in 1927 as a split-off from the already-existing Ozarower society. Aimed to help the needy in Ozarow. Later joined with Ozarower societies in Detroit, Toronto, Montreal to raise relief funds.

Minutes, 1927-59; financial records, 1940's-70's; materials related to anniversary celebrations.

**PIATEGORSK,
PIATIGORY**
Kiev Province,
Ukrainian SSR

164. Piaterer Progressive Benevolent Society, Inc.
    Records, 1926, 1939-1970's, 3" (RG 1085)

Established in 1925; incorporated in 1926. Conducted relief work for home town after WWI; worked through the Russian War Relief to aid *landslayt* during WWII. Built a youth center in Israel.

Certificate of incorporation, 1926; minutes, 1939-67; dues ledger; correspondence; photographs.

Minutes of a meeting, July 8, 1941. (Donated by the Buczacz-American Benevolent Sick and Aid Society)

PINSK
Pinsk province,
Belorussian SSR

165. Congregation Ezras Achim Bnei Pinsk
Records, 1904-1976, 4" (RG 780)

Organized in 1866 for the purpose of establishing a synagogue; incorporated in 1904.

Constitutions; minutes, 1909, 1934-64; financial records, 1908-16, 1931; cemetery maps; correspondence, 1941-76; publication, 1954; souvenir journal of Congregation Dorshei Tov Anshei Pinsk, 1941.

PLOCK
(Rus. Plotsk)
Warszawa province,
Poland

166. Henry Clay Lodge No. 15, Independent Order Brith Abraham
Records, 1890-1947, 12½" (RG 784)

Founded in 1888 by immigrants from Plock as a lodge of the I.O.B.A. Incorporated the Boris Schatz B.S. in 1932 when it appeared the I.O.B.A. would dissolve.

Minutes, 1915-19 (German); financial documents, 1928-47; membership registration book, 1890-99; miscellaneous membership records; 1920-47; correspondence, 1930's; calendar booklets; ballots; announcements; invitations; cemetery maps; *History of the I.O.B.A.*, 1937; constitution, I.O.B.A., 1928; incorporation records of the Boris Schatz B.S., Inc., 1932; photograph; gavels.

167. Plotzker Young Men's Independent Association
Records, 1859, 1918-1973, 12½" (RG 785)

Organized in 1893. Contributed to building a hospital in Plock after WWI. Established a loan fund for *landslayt* in Israel after WWII.

Constitutions; financial documents, 1928-48; membership ledger, 1928-42; cemetery records; speeches; meeting announcements; souvenir journals; calendar booklets, 1920-68; photographs; miscellaneous, 1859, 1920.

PODGAITSY
(Pol. Podhajce)
Ternopol province,
Ukrainian SSR*

168. Congregation Rodef Sholem Independent Podhajcer K.U.V.
Records, 1973-1979, 2½" (RG 1074)

Organized in 1900; owned a synagogue. In later years, met in the Podhajcer synagogue, 108 First Street, New York, owned by another Podhajcer society.

Constitution; minutes, 1977-79; receipts; correspondence.

POGREBISHCHENSK
(until 1945, Pogrebishche)
Vinnitsa province,
Ukrainian SSR

169. First Pogrebisht Benevolent Society, Inc.
Records, 1964-1972, 2½" (RG 1093)

Founded in Brooklyn in 1911. Maintained an emergency fund for needy members; old age fund. Dissolved in the 1970's.

Constitution; financial records, 1964-72; seal.

POLAND

170. American Federation for Polish Jews
Records, 1926, 1938, 1941-1963, 20" (RG 1015)

Formerly known as the Federation of Polish Jews in America. Founded in 1908 as the Federation of Russian-Polish Hebrews, primarily to "help Polish *landslayt* in New York in any possible way" and strengthen the activities of *landsmanshaftn* in the city. Established the Beth David Hospital to aid members and newly-arrived immigrants, c. 1912. Contributed to the People's Relief Committee, 1919. Sent delegate to Versailles Peace Conference, 1919. In 1920, dropped "Russian" from name of organization; in 1926, changed "Hebrews" to "Jews." Established a World Federation of Polish Jews in 1935 for relief and economic assistance for Jews in Poland. The women's division, Ezra, was organized in 1931. Cooperated with the Association of Jewish Refugees and Immigrants from Poland in publishing *The Black Book of Polish Jewry*, 1943. Coordinated relief activities of N.Y. Polish *landsmanshaftn* on behalf of their home towns and *landslayt*, mid-1940's. Actively campaigned against anti-semitism and racial discrimination, 1950's. Organizational leaders included Dr. Joseph Tenenbaum, Zelig Tygel, Benjamin Winter.

Constitution; minutes of committees, 1940's-50's; financial and relief records, 1945-47; records of the Women's Division, 1942-43; organizational reports, 1940's; materials pertaining to membership; correspondence, 1942-63, including correspondence with Austrian organizations (German); materials pertaining to conferences, mass protest meetings, commemorations, 1945-54; materials pertaining to the 4th World Conference of Polish Jews, 1945; testimonies given in Palestine regarding Nazi brutality and escape; reports pertaining to Jewish life in Poland; publications; yearbook, 1938; bulletins; newsletters; typescript chapters of *The Black Book of Polish Jewry*; publicity materials; photographs; materials of the Coordinating Committee of Jewish *Landsmanshaft* Federations.

POLOTSK
Belorussian SSR

171. Polotzker Workingmen's Benevolent Society
Records, 1960-1971, 15" (RG 867)

Organized in 1905. Activities included support of Jewish philanthropies; State of Israel. Dissolved in the 1970's.

Minutes, 1966-69; financial records, 1960's-70's; membership records; correspondence, 1971; stamp.

POVOLOCH
Ukrainian SSR

172. First Povolotcher Sick Benevolent Association
Records, 1942-1977, 2½" (RG 1088)

Organized c. 1907. Maintained a loan fund; supported Israel Bonds; associated with a ladies auxiliary. Dissolved 1977.

Minutes, 1942-75; financial records, 1961-77.

PRAGA WARSZAWSKA
Warszawa province,
Poland

173. Prager-Warschauer Branch 386, Workmen's Circle
Records, 1930-1970, 2½" (RG 1033)

Established in 1915 as a branch of the Workmen's Circle by *landslayt* from the Praga section of Warsaw, emigrating to the U.S. after the 1905 Russian Revolution. Supported the Haym Solomon Warschauer Home for the Aged; relief work for Warsaw. Merged with the Nashelsker Br. 622 W.C., c. 1970.

Minutes, 1968-69; anniversary journals, 1930-65; miscellaneous.

174. First Prager Independent Association, Inc.
Records, 1930-1978, 2½" (RG 1034)

Organized in 1913. Supported the Haym Solomon Warschauer Home for the Aged; was affiliated with the Warschauer Relief, 1920's; the American Council for Warsaw Jews, 1940's. Also worked with its ladies auxiliary.

Constitutions; minutes, 1974-75; financial statements, 1943-48; membership booklets, 1960's; materials pertaining to anniversaries; meeting announcements; secretary's correspondence.

PRILUKI
Chernigov province,
Ukrainian SSR

175. Prudential Benevolent Association, Inc.
Records, 1936-1952, 2½" (RG 974)

Organized in 1899 as the Erster Priluker Society. Adopted constitution in 1918. Later changed name to Prudential B.A., Inc. Lent money to members at low interest rates; provided cemetery grounds; donated to charities.

Constitution; minutes, 1936-52; financial statements; miscellaneous.

A thank you card to delegates Morris and Clara Krugman, who visited Argentina, from a committee of landslayt *in Buenos Aires, preparing to publish a* yisker-bukh *(memorial book) for Zabludowe. (Donated by the Zabludower Yisker Book Committee)*

PROBEZHNA
(Pol. Probuzna)
Ternopol province,
Ukrainian SSR*

176. First Probuzna Sick and Benevolent Society
Records, 1942-1975, 2½" (RG 1017)

Organized and incorporated in 1904.

Certificate of incorporation, 1904; constitution; minutes, 1947-75.

PROSKUROV
Kamenets-Podolski
province,
Ukrainian SSR

177. United Proskurover Relief
Records, 1920-1974, 5" (RG 1083)

Established in 1916 to unite Proskurover *landsmanshaftn* in aid for war victims in Proskurov. Sent delegates to town after pogrom in 1920 to bring relief. Published memorial book to memorialize pogrom victims, 1924. Reestablished in 1939 to work with the United Jewish Appeal to support Palestine. Affiliate organizations were: Proskurover Zion Congregation K.U.V., Proskurov-Yarmolinitzer Br. 355, W.C., New Nook Ass'n., Independent Proskurover Society, Inc. and Sisterhood; First Proskurover Y.M.P.A., Ladies Auxiliary of the First Proskurover, Proskurover, Proskurover Ladies Society, Evans Family Circle.

Record book carried by delegate to Proskurov in 1920 with names of donors and recipients; memorial book, 1924; souvenir journals, 1959-76; taped interviews with delegate, 1979, 1980; records of affiliate organizations: New Nook Association, First Proskurover Y.M.P.A., Proskurover Ladies Benevolent Ass'n., Independent Proskurover Society; photographs.

PRZEMYSL
Rzeszow province,
Poland

178. Congregation Tifereth Joseph Anshei Przemysl
Records, 1917-1967, 7½" (RG 793)

Originally organized in 1891 for the purpose of founding a synagogue; chartered in 1892. Was affiliated with the United Przemysler Relief, organized in 1938 to help *landslayt* in Przemysl.

Constitution (German); certificate of incorporation, 1892; minutes, 1945-65; correspondence, 1930's-40's, also regarding Nazi war crimes testimony and material claims against Germany, 1960's; personal materials relating to Przemysl, 1930's-40's; announcements; anniversary journal, 1941; photographs; memorial book, 1964; materials of the United Relief for Przemysl, 1946.

179. First Przemysler Sick Benefit Society
Records, 1906-1965, 3' 10" (RG 932)

Founded in 1889 to "create a spirit of good fellowship." Maintained a loan fund; supported the Lemberger Home for the Aged, New York.

Constitutions; legal documents, including certificate of incorporation, Przemysler Central Relief Society, Inc., 1919; mintues, 1947-57; cemetery materials; membership records, 1908-64; financial records, 1920-60; photograph; memorial book, 1964.

PYLYAVA
Ukrainian SSR

180. Piliver Podolier Society, Inc.
Records, 1930-1950-1975, 2½" (RG 1068)

Organized in 1915 by 15 *landslayt*. Maintained a loan and old age fund.

Minutes, 1971-75; financial records; souvenir journals, 1930, 1950, 1955; miscellaneous.

RADOM
Kielce province,
Poland

181. First Radomer Congregation, Chebra Agudas Achim Anshei Radom
Records, 1909-1927, 2½" (RG 1038)

Founded in 1903. Maintained a synagogue. Supported the United Radomer Relief for U.S. and Canada, Inc.

Membership applications, c. 1909-27.

182. United Radomer Relief for U.S. and Canada, Inc.
Records, 1947-1979, 2" (RG 813)

Founded in 1917; affiliated with the Radomer Mutual Society, Inc., Radomer Mutual Culture Center which were founded in 1955. Activities include the publication of a newsletter, "Voice of Radom."

Minutes, 1940's-60's; "Voice of Radom," 1965, 67, 68, 72, 76, 79; miscellaneous.

RADOMYSHL
(Pol. Radomysl)
Zhitomir province,
Ukrainian SSR*

183. Radomysler Benevolent Society, Inc.
Records, 1930-1979, 15" (RG 814)

Founded in 1904 as the Radomysler Unterstitzung Verein; changed name to present title and incorporated in 1910. Activities included relief work after WWI and II.

Constitution; minutes, 1930-49; financial records, 1930-79; correspondence; anniversary materials; scrapbook, diary, travel accounts of Samuel Kipnis, 1922-63; publication of the Radomysler Ladies Auxiliary of Chicago; photograph.

RADYMNO
Rzeszow province,
Poland

184. Independent Frymcie Radymnoer Frauen K.U.V.
Records, 1914-1954, 2½" (RG 1050)

Organized in 1905. Also known as the Independent Fremtsche Radimnauer Frauen K.U.V. Dissolved in the 1970's.

Cemetery agreements and permits, 1914-26; membership materials; seal.

RADZYN,
RADZYN PODLASKI
Lublin province,
Poland

185. Radziner Progressive Society, Inc.
Records, 1924-1977, 5" (RG 880)

Founded in 1924. Activities included financial support of the Radziner *landsmanshaft* in Israel.

Minutes, 1924-67, 1973-77; annual reports of Radziner society in Israel, 1968-71, 1974; miscellaneous, including materials pertaining to Radziner society in Israel.

RAIGORODOK, RAYGORODOK
(formerly
Krasny Gorodok)
Stalino province,
Ukrainian SSR

186. First Krasner Sick and Benevolent Society
Records, 1931, 1950-1980, 11" (RG 910)

Founded in Brooklyn in 1905. First meeting was held on Powell Street in the East New York section. Society members ran an independent credit union.

Constitution; minutes, 1950's-70's; membership roster, 1973; correspondence; photograph; tape recording of banquet, 1980.

RASZKOW
(Ger. Raschkow)
Poznan province,
Poland

187. First Rashkower Benevolent Society, Inc.
Records, 1926-1974, 7½" (RG 825)

Founded in 1914; dissolved in 1979.

Constitution; minutes, 1926-34, 1942-50; financial records, 1958-74; burial records; miscellaneous; gavels; banner.

REZEKNE
(Rus., until 1917,
Rezhitsa)
Latvian SSR,
Latvian Republic,
1918-1939

188. Bnai Rezitza Association, Inc.
Records, 1936, 1956-1974, 8" (RG 918)

Founded in 1893; incorporated in 1927. Originally organized to establish a synagogue, located on Forsyth Street, New York. Affiliated with a ladies auxiliary.

Constitution; minutes, 1956-70; financial records; correspondence; cemetery map.

ROGACHEV
(Yid. Ratchev)
Gomel province,
Belorussian SSR

189. Ratchever-Volyner Aid Association, Inc.
Records, 1935-1963, 2½" (RG 992)

Founded in 1914. Established a loan fund; promoted cultural activities. Affiliated with the Ratchever Volyner Froyen Klub, established in 1943 to raise funds for homeless children.

Constitution; minutes, 1935-63; speeches; correspondence; notices.

ROGATIN
(Pol. Rohatyn)
Stanislav province,
Ukrainian SSR*

190. Rohatyner Young Men's Society, Inc.
Records, 1928-1964, 5" (RG 1016)

Organized in 1894.

Constitution; minutes, 1928-60; memorial book, 1962; photograph.

191. Independent Rohatyner Young Men's Benevolent Association
Records, 1953-1977, 1" (RG 1082)

Organized in 1903. Held cultural activities; aided home town. Associated with a ladies auxiliary established in 1934 to help needy *landslayt*.

Minutes, 1965-77; meeting announcements; program.

ROZAN
(Rus. Rozhan)
Warszawa province,
Poland

192. United Rozaner Relief Committee of New York
Records, 1938-1957, 1970's, 2½" (RG 1018)

Founded to aid *landslayt* in Rozan, date unknown. Affiliate organizations included the Rozaner Progressive Y.M.S., Etz Chaim Anshei Rozan, Chassidim Anshei Radzimin, Rozaner Y.F. Br. 544 Workmen's Circle, Rozaner Br. 98, International Worker's Order; Rozaner Ladies B.A. After WWII aided *landslayt* in Displaced Persons Camps and in Israel; Rozaner society in Israel.

Minutes, 1944-57; anniversary journal, 1938; correspondence; membership list of Rozaner Ladies B.A., Inc.

ROZHISHCHE
(Pol. Rozyszcze)
Volyn province,
Ukrainian SSR*

193. First Rozishtcher Benevolent Association
Records, 1925-1976, 2½" (RG 1091)

Founded c. 1912. Maintained a loan fund for members. Dissolved 1976.

Minutes, 1927-35, 1969-76; membership records, 1960's-70's.

RYZHANOVKA
Kiev province,
Ukrainian SSR

194. Riazanifker Benevolent Association, Inc.
Records, 1928-1964, 7½" (RG 882)

Organized in 1913. Activities included working with the ladies auxiliary.

Rules and regulations of the society; minutes, 1941-51; financial records, 1930's-60's; correspondence, 1940's-50's; burial permits, 1928-57.

SADGORA
(Rum. Sadagura)
Chernovtsy province,
Ukrainian SSR
(in Bukovina)

195. Erste Sadagorer Kranken Untershtitzung Verein
Records, 1903-1973, 2½" (RG 917)

Organized in 1903. Provided burial plots for members. Dissolved in the 1970's.

Correspondence and financial records, 1926-73; cemetery records, 1903-59; seal.

SAMBOR
Drogobych province,
Ukrainian SSR*

196. Erster Samborer Kranken Unterstitzung Verein
Records, 1930-1975, 10½" (RG 960)

Founded in 1884; dissolved in 1975.

Certificate of incorporation; minutes, 1930-74 (German); financial records, 1957-66; cemetery records; correspondence; meeting notices; miscellaneous; dissolution ballots.

197. Progressive Samborer Young Men's Benevolent Association
Records, 1910-1977, 5" (RG 796)

Founded in 1910; incorporated in 1915. Formed a *khevre-kedishe* (burial committee) to perform traditional burial rites. Affiliated with the Federation of Polish Jews; with the Erste Samborer K.U.V. Established the United Samborer Relief Society, Inc. (U.S.R.S.), 1937.

Constitutions; minutes, 1937, 1945-46 (German); of the U.S.R.S., 1956; financial documents, 1910, 1930's-60's; legal documents from Sambor; correspondence from Europe, including Sambor, 1912-75; lists of Sambor WWII survivors; journals; bulletins; invitations; newspaper clippings; photographs; draft of history of First Samborer K.U.V., 1889-1975; materials pertaining to the U.S.R.S., United Samborer Orphans Org., Erste Samborer K.U.V., United Samborer Ladies Relief Society, Samborer *landsmanshaft* in Israel; memorial book, 1980.

SATANOV
Kamenets-Podolsk province,
Ukrainian SSR

198. Satanover Benevolent Society
Records, 1903-1972, 13" (RG 818)

Founded in 1903 and chartered in 1904. Organized the Satanover Relief Committee for the War Sufferers to aid *landslayt* during WWI. Sent two delegates to Satanov in 1921 to bring relief and correspondence from American *landslayt*. Aided *landslayt* after WWII; supported Israel.

Constitutions, including that of the Taube Goldstein B.S.; minutes, 1903-38; financial records, 1930's-60's; membership records; records of the Satanover Relief Committee, including correspondence regarding Satanover interned in Austria, Germany, Hungary, 1914-16; correspondence regarding relief work in Satanov, 1921; miscellaneous.

199. Satanover Sisterhood, Inc.
Records, 1943-1970, 5" (RG 819)

Founded in 1931; dissolved and later reestablished in 1954; finally dissolved in 1970. Activities included relief work after WWII and support for Israel. Affiliated with the Satanover B.S.

Certificate of incorporation, 1957; minutes, 1952-70; membership records, 1943-71; announcements; photographs; miscellaneous; seal.

SEKIRYANY
(Yid. Sokorone,
Rum. Secureni)
Chernovtsy province,
Ukrainian SSR
(in Bessarabia)

200. First Sokoroner Dr. Braunstein Progressive Society
Records, 1931-75, 3" (RG 961)

Organized in 1919. Provided lectures and entertainment for members. Benefits included burial. Dissolved in the 1970's.

Minutes, 1951-75; financial records, 1958-75; burial permits, 1931-75; meeting notices; golden book (record of deaths of members); seal; stamps.

SHEPETOVKA
Kamenets-Podolski
province,
Ukrainian SSR

**201. Congregation Bikur Cholim
of East New York (Anshe Shepetovka)**
Records, 1940-1975, 5" (RG 862)

Founded in 1926 by immigrants from Shepetovka; dissolved 1975.

Financial records, including minutes of several meetings, 1937-60; membership records, 1940's-60's; correspondence, 1950's-75; miscellaneous; seal.

Cover from the record book of the Khevre-Kedishe of the Schklover Untershtitzungs Verein. (Donated by the Schklover Independent Benevolent Association, Inc.)

SHKLOV
Mogilev province,
Belorussian SSR

202. Schklover Independent Benevolent Association, Inc.
Records, 1896-1974, 1'6" (RG 848)

Incorporated in 1918 as the Schklover Auxiliary Society, Inc. Affiliated with the Khevre Kedishe Schklover U.V., established 1893, also known as the Khevre Kedishe Anshey Shklover. Society changed name legally in 1947 to Schklover Ind. B.A., Inc. The Khevre Kedishe established a loan fund in 1905 which became property of the society in 1927.

Certificate of incorporation, 1918; legal documents; constitution; minutes, 1951-71; financial records, 1918-60, 1973-74; materials pertaining to membership, 1914-50's; correspondence; materials pertaining to burial and endowments; record book of the Khevre Kedishe.

SKALA
Ternopol province,
Ukrainian SSR*

203. Skalar Benevolent Society
Records, 1931-1946, 1978, 1980, 3" (RG 1039)

Organized in 1893, splitting off from an older group. Constitution states that the society cannot affiliate with a lodge or synagogue except on the consent of ⅔ of the membership or support political or economic matters.

Constitution; anniversary journals, 1938-41, 1946; memorial book, 1978; taped interview with ex-officer.

SKIDEL
Grodno province,
Belorussian SSR*

204. Skidler Benevolent Association
Records, 1928, 1933, 1956-1974, 2½" (RG 1019)

Founded in 1900. Established a relief committee after WWI; sent a delegate with funds to Skidel in 1921.

Constitution; minutes, 1956-1974; financial papers, 1962-64; anniversary journal, photographs; miscellaneous.

SKIERNIEWICE
Lodz province,
Poland

205. Independent Skierniewicer Benevolent Association
Records, 1913-1963, 10" (RG 811)

Founded in 1913. Organized the Skierniewicer Relief Committee for aid to the home town in WWI. Established the Skierniewicer Patronat in the 1930's to free political prisoners in Skierniewice. In 1937, the Relief Committee and the Patronat joined to form the United Relief Committee for Skierniewice. Established a *gmileskhesed kase* (free loan fund) in 1955 for *landslayt* in Israel.

Minutes, 1913-58; anniversary journals; memorial book, 1955; photographs; newspaper clippings; film of memorial service in Skierniewice, 1947.

SMELA
Kiev province,
Ukrainian SSR

See Cherkassy-Smela Benevolent Association, Inc., entry 41.

SMOLEVICHI
Minsk province,
Belorussian SSR

206. United Smolewitzer Association, Inc.
Records, 1921-1974, 2'3½" (RG 849)

Organized in 1920; chartered in 1922. Established a Russian Relief Fund in WWII and contributed to relief efforts after the War. Dissolved 1974.

Minutes, 1921-32, 1940-74; financial records, 1940's-70's; correspondence, 1953-74; miscellaneous; seal; stamp.

SNYATYN
(Pol. Sniatyn),
Stanislav province,
Ukrainian SSR*

207. Paul Revere Lodge No. 464, Independent Order Brith Abraham
Records, 1936-1968, 5" (RG 829)

Founded in 1908. In the 1930's was called the Sniatyner Lodge 464, later changing its name to the Paul Revere Lodge No. 464, I.O.B.A. Founded a loan fund, 1912; sick benefit fund, 1915.

Minutes, 1936-68; minutes of the Sniatyner American Lodge, Inc., 1941-51; anniversary journal, 1958.

SOLY
Vilna province,
Belorussian SSR*

208. Soler Brothers Benevolent Association
Records, 1956-1974, 2½" (RG 940)

Organized in 1903. Sent aid to Soly. Active until 1974.

Financial records.

SOPOTSKIN
(Pol. Sopockine)
Grodno province,
Belorussian SSR*

See Congregation Achei Grodno Vasapotkin and Chevra Mishnayos, entry 66.

SOROKI
(Rum. Soroca)
Moldavian SSR
(in Bessarabia)

209. Soroker Young Friends Benevolent and Educational League
Records, 1921-1975, 1'8½" (RG 831)

Originally founded in 1910 as a single men's club, but was soon opened to women as members married. Briefly united with the Uriver branch of the Workmen's Circle, but left before WWI. Worked with other Soroker organizations, including the First Soroker Mutual Aid Society, First Soroker Ladies Bessarabier Society, the Young Women's League of the Soroker Young Friends B.S.

Constitutions; minutes, 1921-47, 1950, 1952-64, 1974-75; rulings and recommendations, special committees, 1930-57; financial records; journal, Bessarabian Federation of American Jews, Inc.; photographs; miscellaneous; velvet vestments with medallions worn by officers; pennants; banner.

210. First Soroker Bessarabier Mutual Aid Society
Records, 1910-1950's, 1'1" (RG 832)

Founded in 1897. Activities included extensive relief work for the home town in the 1920's and 30's and for *landslayt* in Israel in the 1950's. Worked with the Soroker Relief in the U.S., a central organization composed of: First Soroker Mutual Aid, Soroker Young Friends B.E.L., First Soroker Bess. Ladies. Merged in the 1930's with the Seltzer Lodge. Supported the Bessarabian Federation of American Jews after WWII.

Pinkes (record book) of the *khevre-kedishe* (burial committee), 1910-53, including minutes, rules, names of officers and deceased society members; golden book (record of deaths of members); materials from Soroki relating to relief activities of American *landslayt*, 1920's-30's; memorial book of Jewish hospital in Soroki, 1922; materials pertaining to trip of Morris Seltzer to Soroki for distribution of relief funds, 1925; personal materials, book of memoirs of home town by David Seltzer; correspondence; anniversary jounals; endowment fund report; photographs of Soroki, 1920's-30's; constitution, First Soroker Bess. Ladies Aid Society; materials pertaining to the Bessarabian Federation of American Jews; address list, First Soroker Ladies Aid Society.

STANISLAV
Stanislav province,
Ukrainian SSR*

211. Stanislauer Progressive Benevolent Association
Records, 1917-1973, 5" (RG 920)

Founded in 1916. During and after WWI participated in the Stanislauer Relief, together with the First Stanislauer Y.M.B.A. and the Ershte Knihinin Stanislauer K.U.V. to aid *landslayt* in the home town. Dissolved in the 1970's.

Financial records, 1950's-70's; membership applications, 1917-61; miscellaneous.

STARAYA USHITSA
(Yid. Ushitse Podolye)
Kamenets-Podolski province,
Ukrainian SSR

212. First Ushitzer Podoler Benevolent Association, Inc.
Records, 1913-1971, 3" (RG 1084)

Organized in 1911; incorporated in 1913 to aid *landslayt* in New York and in the home town.

Certificate of incorporation, mounted on decorative panel, 1913; golden book (record of deaths of members); banner.

STAWISKI
(Rus. Staviski)
Bialystok province,
Poland

213. Stavisker Young Men's Benevolent Association
Records, 1911-1973, 1'3" (RG 850)

Organized in 1908. Provided disability benefits and loans to members. Affiliated with the Stavisker Ladies Aid Society. Dissolved in the 1970's.

Minutes, 1939-72; financial records, 1930's-70's; correspondence; seal.

STOLIN
Pinsk province,
Belorussian SSR*

214. Stoliner Progressive Society, Inc.
Records, 1935-1973, 12½" (RG 847)

Organized in 1919. Affiliated with Stoliner branches of the Workmen's Circle. Supported charities; the local Hebrew School.

Minutes, 1940-73; financial records, 1950's-70's; burial permits; miscellaneous; seal; stamps.

STOPNICA
(Yid. Stopnits)
Kielce province,
Poland

215. Stopnitzer Young Men's Benevolent Association
Records, 1911-1921, 1945, 5" (RG 915)

Founded in 1905. Sent funds to Stopnits after WWI and established a Stopnitzer Relief in WWII. Was affiliated with a ladies auxiliary which dissolved in the 1970's.

Minutes, 1911-21; photographs; miscellaneous.

216. Chevra Oir Lashumaim Anshei Stopnitz
Records, 1925-1947, 2½" (RG 916)

Founded in 1925 and met in a synagogue located at 81 Columbia Street, New York. Moved to 122 Columbia Street, 1935.

Minutes, 1925-47.

STOROZHINETS
Chernovtsy province,
Ukrainian SSR
(Bukovina)

217. First Independent Storoznetzer Bukowiner Sick and Benevolent Association
Records, 1904-1977, 7½" (RG 901)

Organized in 1903 and incorporated in 1904. Established a war relief committee during WWI. Also maintained a relief committee and a Ladies of the War Relief during WWII. Sent relief funds and packages to *landslayt* in Europe and Israel.

Certificate of incorporation, 1904; constitution; minutes, 1911, 1946-53; financial records, 1948-76; materials pertaining to burial, 1904-77; souvenir journals; meeting announcements; photographs.

Photograph of a carriage from the livery of Josef Schwartz, co-founder of Hirsch & Schwartz, which rented hearses and carriages to landsmanshaftn *for funerals. (Donated by Jacob Schwartz, Schwartz Brothers Memorial Chapel, Inc.)*

STRY
(Pol. Stryj)
Drogobych province,
Ukrainian SSR*

218. First Stryjer Sisters Benevolent Society
Records, 1950-1968, 5" (RG 863)

Founded in 1904. Organized to provide burial for women from Stryj. Dissolved 1968.

Minutes, 1953-1968; financial records, 1950's-60's; membership records, 1952-68.

SVISLOCH
(Pol. Swislocz)
Grodno province,
Belorussian SSR*

219. Swislotcher Benevolent Association
Records, 1917-1971, 7½" (RG 921)

Founded in 1912. Aided *landslayt* in Swislocz after WWI. Maintained a loan fund for members.

Constitution; minutes, 1928-47; financial records; correspondence; membership applications; burial permits.

SZCZENIEC
Nowogrodek province,
Belorussian SSR*

220. Szenicer Ladies Sick and Benevolent Society
Records, 1942-1972, 10" (RG 875)

Organized to provide sick and death benefits for its female members. Activities included the organization of a *shive* (seven days of mourning) committee. Dissolved 1974.

Financial records, 1940's-70's; cemetery book; miscellaneous.

A farewell to Rose Schwartz by the committee of an orphanage in Paris supported by the World Federation of Bessarabian Jews, 1950. (Donated by Rose Schwartz)

SZTABIN
Bialystok province,
Poland

221. Stabiner Young Men's Benevolent Association
Records, 1907-1928, 1947, 2½" (RG 1037)

Founded in 1907 to unite *landslayt* in one society. Dissolved 1976.

Minutes, 1907-28; miscellaneous, including doctors' notes, 1920's, 1947.

SZYDLOWIEC
(Rus. Shidlovets)
Kielce province,
Poland

222. Shedlowtzer Benevolent Association
Records, 1910-1980, 5" (RG 894)

Founded in 1909 as the Shidlovtser Untershtitsung Fareyn. Was affiliated with the Shedlowtzer Ladies Society (est'd. 1925), Shedlowtzer Junior League (est'd. 1934). Neither exist today. Established an old age fund to help members over the age of 65, 1924. Aided *landslayt* and communal institutions especially in years of WWI. Published memorial book in 1974 with cooperation of committees of Shidlovtser *landslayt* in Israel. Support Jewish institutions and charities in New York and Israel.

Minutes, 1910-13, 1943-65; souvenir journals; meeting announcements; photograph; photocopy of autobiography submitted to YIVO (Vilna) autobiography contest, 1934.

TARNOW
Krakow province,
Poland

223. Independent Tarnower Kranken Unterstuetzungs Verein
Records, 1946-1973, 2½" (RG 1069)

Organized before 1917 to aid the sick and needy.

Constitution; membership application book, 1946-71 (older application forms in German).

TEREBOVLYA
(Pol. Trembowla)
Ternopol province,
Ukrainian SSR*

224. Trembowla True Sisters, Inc.
Records, 1921-1965, 2" (RG 794)

Founded in 1918 to assist *landslayt* in Trembowla in the aftermath of WWI. Members and officers consist almost exclusively of women.

Invitations; personal legal documents; photographs.

225. Congregation Agudas Achim Anshei Trembowla K.U.V.
Records, 1908, 1925-1948, 5½" (RG 1070)

Founded in 1901. Provided aid to home town institutions; sent a delegate to Trembowla with relief funds after WWI. Maintained a synagogue on Houston Street, New York.

Constitution, 1908; minutes, 1931-48; financial ledger, 1925-34.

226. Erste Trembowler Kranken Unterstitzung Verein
Records, 1957-1968, 1" (RG 1073)

Founded in 1897 with 7 members. Dissolved 1968.

Minutes, 1957-68; seal.

TIMKOVICHI
Bobruisk province,
Belorussian SSR

227. Congregation Ahavath Zedek Anshei Timkowitz
Records, 1906-1965, 8" (RG 840)

Incorporated in 1892. Had its own synagogue on Henry Street, New York. At one time worked with an affiliated ladies auxiliary.

Minutes; 1906-19; financial records, 1930's-60's; *gmiles-khesed* (loan fund) certificates, 1944-64, receipts, 1954-65.

TOUSTE
Ternopol province,
Ukrainian SSR*

228. Erste Tauster Unterstutzung Verein
Records, 1899-1974, 4" (RG 1089)

Established in 1898 and incorporated in 1899 to promote "the benevolent instincts of the members and to do religious worship according to the Hebrew faith." Contributed to Jewish philanthropies.

Certificate of incorporation, 1899; constitution; financial records; cemetery materials; correspondence; agreement between society and meeting hall, 1903 (German).

TULCHIN
Vinnitsa province,
Ukrainian SSR

229. Tolchiner Benevolent Society
Records, 1933-1952, 10" (RG 838)

Founded in 1895 and chartered in 1897. Associated with a ladies auxiliary.

Minutes, 1942-52; financial records, 1933-51; miscellaneous; cemetery map.

TURISK
(Pol. Turzysk)
Volyn province,
Ukrainian SSR*

230. Trisker Voliner Young Men's Benevolent Association
Records, 1923-1972, 10" (RG 914)

Founded in 1915. Engaged in relief work and support of the needy in Trisk between the two world wars; supported the *folkshul* (public school) there. After WWII, sent clothing and food packages to survivors.

Constitution; minutes, 1923-36; financial records; correspondence; cemetery map; memorial book, 1975; memoir, 1976; gavel.

UKRAINE
constituent republic,
SW European USSR

231. National Jewish Ukrainian Committee of the Jewish Council for Russian War Relief
Records, 1943-1946, 1" (RG 1079)

Organized mid-1940's to mobilize Jewish Ukrainian *landsmanshaftn* in the United States to raise relief and rehabilitation funds for *landslayt*, to be distributed through the Jewish Council for Russian War Relief. Led by Rabbi Abraham Bick, president.

Minutes, 1945; correspondence, relief reports, contribution lists, 1943-46.

ULLA
Vitebsk province,
Belorussian SSR

232. Uller Benevolent Association
Records, 1950-1977, 2½" (RG 1086)

Organized in 1906 to aid *landslayt* and for social purposes. Dissolved 1977.

Minutes; receipt book, 1966-77; materials pertaining to dissolution; correspondence; cemetery map; seal.

USCIE ZIELONE
Ternopol province,
Ukrainian SSR*

233. First Uscie Zielone Sick and Benevolent Association
Records, 1911, 1930-1964, 5" (RG 845)

Established and incorporated in 1911. Maintained synagogue on Ridge Street, New York. Society split in 1926, leading to the establishment of a second association, the First American Uscie Zielone Sick Support Society.

Certificate of incorporation, 1911; minutes, 1930-48; financial records, 1940-63.

USTILUG
(Pol. Uscilug)
Volyn province,
Ukrainian SSR*

234. First Austiler Aid Society
Records, 1940's-1971, 2" (RG 1005)

Chartered as The First Austiler Aid Society in New York, 1911. Was affiliated with the United Austiler Relief Committee which raised money for *landslayt* after WWII.

Constitution; minutes, 1968-71; memorial journal, United Austiler Relief Committee, 1948; theater programs, Ustilug, pre-WWII.

Independent Skierniewicer Benevolent Association, New York, holds yisker *(memorial) meeting, lighting candles for the six million Jews killed in the Holocaust. Chelsea Hall, 1979. (Photographer: Ricki Rosen)*

VASHKOVTSY
(Rum. Vasckauti)
Chernovtsy province,
Ukrainian SSR
(in Bukovina)

235. First Washkoutz Bucowinaer Sick and Benevolent Society
Records, 1926, 1950's, 5" (RG 993)

Founded in 1903. Contributed to Jewish philanthropies. Conducted extensive relief work for *landslayt* in Israel in the 1950's.

Constitution; financial records, 1954-56; relief work records, including correspondence with *landslayt* and records of packages sent; membership lists; correspondence; miscellaneous.

VILEIKA, VILEYKA
Molodechno province,
Belorussian SSR*

236. Vileika Aid Association of Lynn, Massachusetts
Records, 1915-1957, 1½" (RG 1072)

Established in Lynn, Mass., 1915; incorporated in 1916 for the purpose of "aiding, assisting, and relieving the poor and needy people of the Jewish faith." Engaged in extensive relief work for the home town after WWI.

Certificate of incorporation, 1916; minutes and by-laws, 1915-55; correspondence; correspondence and reports from institutions in Vileika regarding relief, including the Vileiker Jewish Committee, Jewish Relief Committee (YEKOPO), 1919-30.

VIZHNITSA
Chernovtsy province,
Ukrainian SSR
(in Bukovina)

237. First Wiznitz Bukawinaer Ladies Society, Inc.
Records, 1938-1966, 10" (RG 852)

Organized in 1921 as the First Wiznitz Bucowiner Ladies Benevolent Ass'n., Inc. Changed name to present title legally in 1923. Society now dissolved.

Minutes, 1956-66; seal.

An ambulance for Israel, donated through the Kittever Ladies Relief Auxiliary, New York, 1968. (Donated by the Ray Heit Chapter of the Kittever Ladies Relief Auxiliary)

VOINILOV, VOYNILOV
(Pol. Wojnilow)
Stanislav province,
Ukrainian SSR*

238. First Wojnilower Sick Benevolent Society
Records, 1913-1977, 1'5½" (RG 834)

Founded in 1905. Merged with the First Wojnilower Lodge No. 674, Independent Order Brith Abraham, established in 1913.

Constitution; minutes, of the First Wojnilower Lodge, 1913-17; of the First Wojnilower S.B.S., 1917-77; of the gate committee, 1956-71; financial records of both societies, 1913-54; correspondence, 1940's-60's; newspaper clippings.

VOLKOVYSK
(Pol. Wolkowysk)
Grodno province,
Belorussian SSR*

239. Wolkowysker Relief Society
Records, 1920-1922, 1" (RG 1042)

Founded in 1917 to bring relief to *landslayt* in Wolkowysk. Headquartered in the Wolkowysker synagogue at 28 Pike Street, New York. Sent delegates to home town with relief funds in 1920, 1921. Dissolved 1923.

Record book of trip to Wolkowysk, kept by relief delegate, Harry Nachimoff; passport and personal materials pertaining to delegates H. Nachimoff, Abraham Berg; photographs, miscellaneous.

240. Congregation Adath Wolkowisk of Brownsville
Records, 1911-1933, 5" (RG 981)

Organized in Brooklyn in 1911 to provide members with free loans, cemetery plots, synagogue for study and prayer. From 1911 to 1938 relocated synagogue from Stone Avenue to Christopher Street to Osborn Street, to Sackman Street, Brooklyn.

Materials pertaining to congregational regulations; minutes, 1911-13, 1919-31; financial records, 1920's-30's; membership records; materials pertaining to synagogue activities.

WARSAW
Warszawa province,
Poland

241. Warschauer Benevolent Society, Inc.
Records, 1941-1970, 5" (RG 1020)

Founded in 1906. Organized a Young Group in 1932 to attract younger members. Established a relief committee for European Jews in 1946. Worked with the society's ladies auxiliary to send relief and food packages to needy *landslayt* in Europe. Supported the Warschauer Haym Solomon Home for the Aged.

Constitution; minutes, 1944-70; materials pertaining to burial; monthly bulletins; miscellaneous, including membership directories.

242. American Council for Warsaw Jews (American Council of Warsaw Jews)
Records, 1943-1947, 1" (RG 1041)

Established in 1942 to "aid Jews in Warsaw and outlying cities; to give immediate aid to Warsaw Jews wherever they can be reached; to help the post-war reconstruction of the Warsaw Jewish community; to aid and centralize activities of Warsaw Jews in America." Sent delegates to Warsaw. Dissolved 1950's.

Membership records; organizational records, including some minutes, 1943; memoir by delegate Samuel Wohl, 1947 (Yiddish); press releases; correspondence; resolutions.

WLOCLAWEK
Bydgoszcz province,
Poland

243. Associated Benevolent Young Men, Inc.
Records, 1937-1974, 7½" (RG 930)

Established in 1907 as the Independent Woltzlawker Young Men's Benevolent Society, Inc. Associated with Congregation Ahavas Achim Wloslawek, established 1881. Affiliated with the Federation of Polish Jews in America. Changed name to present title, 1945.

Certificate of name change, 1945; constitution; minutes, 1949-73; financial records, 1963-76; materials pertaining to burial; materials pertaining to membership; correspondence; meeting notices; seal; materials of Wloclawker Chebra Ahabath Achim.

YAVOROV
(Pol. Jaworow)
Lvov province,
Ukrainian SSR*

244. Independent Jaworower Association
Records, 1932-1962, 8" (RG 967)

Founded in 1913 to provide the younger Jaworower *landslayt* with an alternative to the older, more religious Erste Jaworower Kranken Unterstitzung Verein. The two societies merged in 1948.

Minutes, 1932-49 (Yiddish, German); of the Erste Jaworower K.U.V., 1921-38; financial materials; memorial book, 1956.

ZABLUDOW
Bialystok province,
Poland

245. Zabludower Yisker Book Committee
Records, 1925, 1928, 1961, 2½" (RG 1031)

Established in Buenos Aires to publish a memorial book commemorating the destroyed town and exterminated inhabitants of Zabludow during WWII. Members of the Zabludower K.U.V. in New York participated in the publication.

Memorial book, 1961; materials used in preparation; citation; journals, 1925, 1928.

ZALESHCHIKI
(Pol. Zaleszczyki)
Ternopol province,
Ukrainian SSR*

246. Zaleszczyker Kranken Untershtitsungs Verein
Records, 1954-1976, 3" (RG 1094)

Organized in 1891; provided aid for *landslayt*. Dissolved 1977.

Financial records, 1970-75; miscellaneous, including papers pertaining to dissolution; seal.

ZAREMBY,
ZAREBY KOSCIELNE
Bialystok province,
Poland

247. Zaromber Israel Aid Society
Records, 1926-1965, 2½" (RG 965)

Founded in 1937 as the Zaromber Relief Committee to economically assist *landslayt* and institutions in Zaremby. Also known as the United Zaromber Relief Committee. Worked through the Joint Distribution Committee (J.D.C.), 1930's. Dedicated monument in Zaremby to Holocaust victims.

Correspondence and reports from Zaremby and the J.D.C., 1930's; bulletins, 1926-65; souvenir journal, 1965; tape recordings (2), made in Zaremby at the dedication of a monument, sponsored by a committee of the Zaromber Relief immediately after WWII.

ZAWICHOST
Kielce province,
Poland

248. First Zawichoster Young Men's Benevolent Association
Records, 1914-1953, 2½" (RG 964)

Founded in 1913 to provide *landslayt* with "spiritual and material benefits." Conducted relief work for home town after WWI.

Minutes, 1941-53; anniversary journal, 1931; photographs.

ZBARAZH
(Pol. Zbaraz)
Ternopol province,
Ukrainian SSR*

249. First Zbarazer Relief Society
Records, 1943-1977, 5" (RG 982)

Founded in 1925. Between the two world wars, aided communal institutions in Zbaraz. After WWII, aided survivors in relocating and establishing themselves in the U.S.

Minutes, 1943-77 (German, English); financial records; membership records, 1946-73.

Map of Brzezin (Brzeziny) drawn by Yudel Fuchs-Krayndls for the Brzezin memorial book. (Donated by the Brzeziner Sick and Benevolent Society, Inc.)

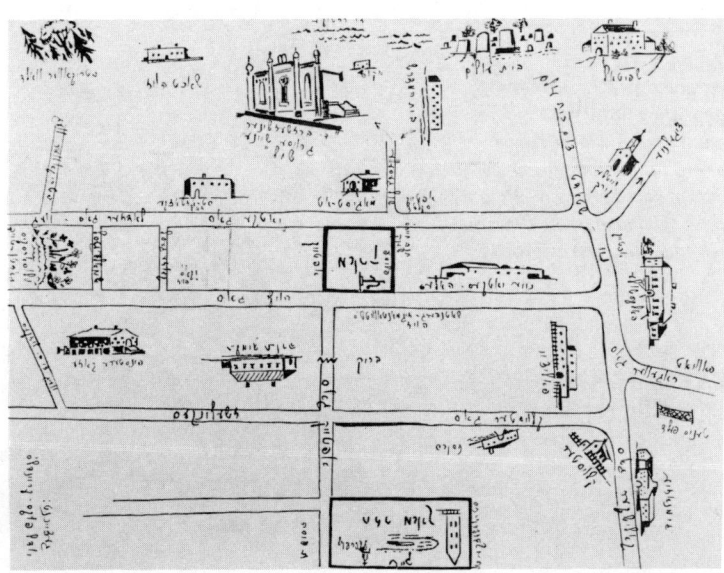

ZBOROV
(Pol. Zborow)
Ternopol province,
Ukrainian SSR*

250. First Zborower Sick and Benevolent Association
Records, 1934-1978, 11" (RG 798)

Founded in 1896 to establish a synagogue and provide mutual aid.

Constitutions; financial reports; membership ledgers; souvenir journal, 1934; meeting announcements; newspaper clippings.

ZDUNSKA WOLA
Lodz province,
Poland

251. First Zdunska Wola Benevolent Society
Records, 1902, 1915-1977, 6" (RG 808)

Founded in 1902. Activities included relief work during WWI and after WWII; the establishment of a credit union in Israel; the erection of Holocaust monuments in Israel and Zdunska Wola; affiliation with the American Federation for Aid to Polish Jews; support for the Reuben Brainin Children's Clinic, Tel-Aviv, Israel.

Incorporation charter, 1902; minutes, 1928-37; financial records, 1951-55; anniversary journal, 1952; correspondence; miscellaneous materials relating to the Committee for the Reuben Brainin Clinic in Israel, the American Federation for Aid to Polish Jews; photographs.

ZELECHOW
Warszawa province,
Poland

252. First Zelechover Progressive Society
Records, 1944-1974, 5" (RG 1025)

Founded in 1900's; original purpose included establishment of a synagogue. Split over political rifts in the 1920's and fell apart soon after. Was reestablished by WWII survivors, 1951. Chicago *landsmanshaft* published monthly bulletins to unite scattered Zelechover *landslayt*, an autobiographical volume by Y. M. Weissenberg, a memorial book.

Minutes; expense book for Weissenberg book fund; publications, 1940's-60's; membership list, New York society; photographs.

Brzeziner WWII survivors honor their landslayt *(countrymen) who perished during the liquidation of the Brzezin ghetto, Brzezin, Poland, 1947. (Donated by the Brzeziner Sick and Benevolent Society)*

ZGIERZ
Lodz province,
Poland

253. Zgierzer Sick Benevolent Society
Records, 1903-1914, 2" (RG 1064)

A mutual aid society founded by former residents of Zgierz. No other information available.

Minutes, 1904-14, including minutes of the Zdinskawolla Lodge 131, Independent Order Free Sons of Judah, 1903.

ZGURITSA
Moldavian SSR
(Bessarabia)

254. Zguritzer-Bessarabier Society
Records, 1925-1974, 3" (RG 1080)

Founded before 1921. Associated with a ladies auxiliary established to raise money for charities.

Minutes, 1925-74.

ZHASHKOV
Kiev province,
Ukrainian SSR

255. Zashkover Kranken Untershtitzung Verein of New York
Records, 1934-1970, 10" (RG 884)

Organized in 1914. Activities included the establishment of a free loan fund for its members. Zashkover Ladies Auxiliary founded 1923; its presidents were appointed by the Zashkover K.U.V. Provided relief for *landslayt* after WWI and II; support for Israel. Maintained contact with the Zashkover U.V. and Ladies Auxiliary of Philadelphia and with the Zashkover Aid Society of Boston.

Constitution; minutes, 1938-61; financial records, 1949-66; correspondence, 1948-70; anniversary journals; miscellaneous.

ZHVANCHIK
Kamenets-Podolski
province,
Ukrainian SSR

256. Zwantchyker Podolier Young Men's Benevolent Association, Inc.
Records, 1936-1974, 4" (RG 1075)

Established in 1913. Maintained an old age and disability fund; also founded a Zwantchyker Relief Fund. Associated with a ladies auxiliary established in 1936.

Constitution; minutes, 1952-74; ledger; journal, 1938; photographs.

ZHVANETS
Kamenets-Podolski
province,
Ukrainian SSR

257. Zwanitz Podolier Progressive Branch 277, Workmen's Circle and Zwanitz Podolier Relief Committee, Inc.
Records, 1905-1959, 2½" (RG 1026)

Established in 1909 as the Zwanitz Podolier Progressive Society; accepted that same year into the Workmen's Circle as Branch 277 (In 1930, some members broke away to form the Podolier Br. 277, International Workers' Order). Zwanitzer *landslayt* from all societies united in 1944 to form the Zwanitz Podolier Relief Committee to aid surviving *landslayt* after WWII.

Records of Br. 277: anniversary journals; materials of the Relief Committee, yearbook; 1946; notices; miscellaneous; photographs.

ZINKOW
Kamenets-Podolski province,
Ukrainian SSR

258. First Independent Zinkower Society
Records, 1952-1975, 3" (RG 962)

Founding date unknown. Provided burial and funeral expenses. Dissolved 1976.

Minutes, 1973-76; financial records, 1952-74; cemetery map.

259. Zinkower Podolier Benevolent Association
Records, 1924-1974, 5" (RG 963)

Founded in 1909, two years after a previously organized Zinkover society had dissolved. Relief activities included sending packages through the Russian War Relief to the home town. After WWII, helped sponsor publication of a memorial book and erection of a monument in memory of Holocaust victims.

Certificate of incorporation, 1924; constitution; minutes, 1939-58; correspondence; memoirs of Zinkow; materials relating to Holocaust commemoration in Zinkow; photographs; miscellaneous.

ZINKOWITZ
Kamenets-Podolski province,
Ukrainian SSR

260. Zinkowitzer & Kamenetz Podolier Society, Inc.
Records, 1952-1970's, 2½" (RG 1066)

Established in 1963-64 by a merger of the First Zinkowitzer Podolier K.U.V. (est'd. c. 1904) and the Kamenetzer Podolier B.A. Paid *shive* (seven days of mourning) benefits.

Minutes, 1963-75; of the First Zinkowitzer Pod. K.U.V., 1956-64; correspondence, 1970's; Kamenetz-Podolsk memorial book, 1960; bulletins of the Kamenetzer Podolier B.A.

ZUROW
Stanislav province,
Ukrainian SSR*

261. Chevra Bnei Israel Anshei Zurow
Records, 1934-1964, 2" (RG 1077)

Founded in 1896 to provide members with a place to pray. Also known as the Chevra Bnei Israel Anshei Zurow Galician, Inc.

Minutes, 1934-64, including burial permits.

ZYRARDOW
Warszawa province,
Poland

262. Klub Zyrardow
Records, 1909, 1920-1977, 2½" (RG 801)

Organized by Leo Feld in 1963 for the purpose of publishing a memorial book on Zyrardow. Activities include erecting a monument for Holocaust victims and reconstruction and maintenance of the Jewish cemetery in Zyrardow.

Correspondence pertaining to *landslayt*, 1920's, 1952-58; the *Pinkes* (record book), 1963-72; speeches; autobiographical materials; miscellaneous materials relating to the Zyrardow Br. 301, Workmen's Circle, Zyrardow *landsmanshaft* in Israel.

SECTION B: NON-LOCALITY BASED SOCIETY RECORDS

263. Abraham Cohen Benevolent Society, Inc.
Records, 1919, 1954-1973, 1" (RG 1008)

Incorporated in 1919. Held annual memorial meetings for deceased members. Dissolved 1973.

Certificate of incorporation, 1919; minutes, 1954-72; materials pertaining to dissolution, 1973.

264. Chevra Kadisha Beth Israel
Records, 1914-1967, 12½" (RG 865)

A fraternal organization providing sick and death benefits for its members. The society was founded in 1858, closed to new members in 1948 and disbanded in 1967.

Minutes, 1943-67; financial records, 1943-67; membership records, 1920-67; burial permits, 1914-66; correspondence, 1950's-60's; announcements; cemetery map; seal.

265. David Kantrowitz Family Benevolent Association (DKFBA)
Records, 1921-1979, 1" (RG 1059)

Incorporated in 1909 by descendents of Russian-born Mirke (Miriam) Becker to unite her lineal descendents by blood or marriage; aid members; commemorate memory of departed members. Gave free loans; contributed to charities.

Constitution; *DKFBA Golden Book and Family Register,* 1979; family magazine, 1925; souvenir handkerchief of relative's funeral, 1921.

266. Deborah Rebekah Lodge No. 13, Independent Order of Odd Fellows
Records, 1912-1926, 1971-1975, 11" (RG 958)

A lodge of the Rebekah Assembly of the I.O.O.F. Conducted social and charitable activities; contributed to Jewish philanthropies.

Minutes, 1971-75; financial ledger, 1912-26 (German); certificates; banners (4); capes.

267. Dora Lipkowitz Voluntary Aid and Sick Benefit Society
Records, 1970-1976, 2½" (RG 953)

Founding date unknown. Provided cemetery benefits for members. Dissolved 1976.

Minutes; materials pertaining to burial and finances; seal.

268. Empire State Lodge No. 460, Independent Order of Odd Fellows
Records, 1936-1977, 7½" (RG 873)

A fraternal lodge of the I.O.O.F. Share common cemetery grounds with the Empire Fellowship Association, Sochrochiner Lodge, Independent Sochrochiner B.A., Shevas Israel Anshe Raigod in the Washington Cemetery, Brooklyn.

By-laws of lodge; minutes, 1950-53; 1959-77; membership records, 1930's, 40's, 60's, 70's.

269. Family Lodge No. 189, Independent Order Brith Abraham
Records, 1935-1955, 2½" (RG 830)

Founding date unknown. A lodge in the Independent Order Brith Abraham fraternal order.

Financial records; correspondence, 1953-55.

270. Goldfaden Camp No. 9, Order Bnai Zion
Records, 1906-1951, 10" (RG 1065)

Founded in 1908 as the Abraham Goldfaden Zion Camp No. 9, a branch of the Order Sons of Zion (Bnai Zion). Provided members with insurance, death benefits, social and cultural activities. Camp No. 9 was associated wtih a ladies auxiliary.

Constitution; minutes, 1914-32; financial records, 1929-36; membership materials, 1939; correspondence; materials pertaining to Bnai Zion and other chapters, including the Bistritz & Vicinity Chapter 33.

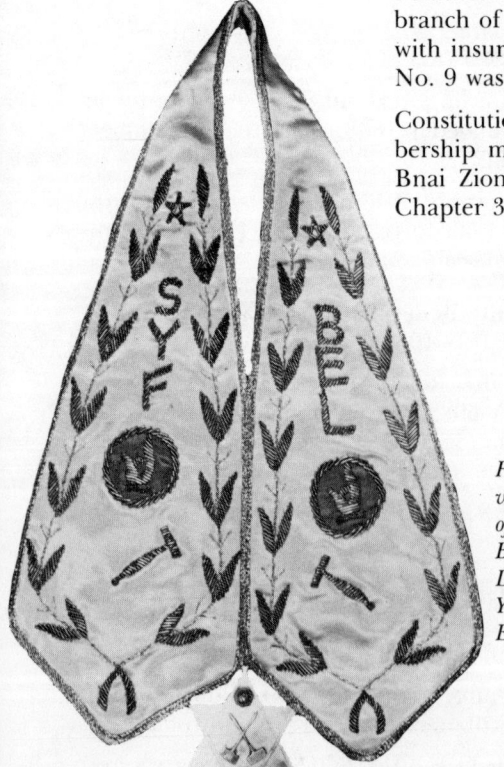

Hand-embroidered velvet vestment worn by the President of the Soroker Young Friends Benevolent and Educational League. (Donated by the Soroker Young Friends Benevolent and Educational League)

271. Hatikvo Beneficial Society, Inc.
Records, 1917, 1930-1975, 5" (RG 986)

Incorporated in 1917. Took over the cemetery property of the Mordecai Lodge No. 24, Order Brith Abraham in Washington Cemetery, Brooklyn, 1917. Dissolved in the 1970's.

Certificate of incorporation, 1917; dissolution form; minutes, 1952-56; financial records, 1950's; materials pertaining to burial, including cemetery deed between society and the Mordecai Lodge No. 24, O.B.A., 1917.

272. Independent Brodsky Benevolent Association, Inc.
Records, 1941-1974, 5" (RG 979)

Organized in 1900 as the Lazar I. Brodsky Lodge No. 258, Independent Order Brith Abraham. Later changed name to Ind. Brodsky B.A., Inc., but maintained contact with I.O.B.A. Dissolved 1975.

Minutes, 1941-57; financial records, 1950-74.

273. Khevre Kol Ahavas Khayim
Records, 1949-1970; 2½" (RG 978)

Owned synagogue at 592 Marcy Street, Brooklyn where the *khevre* met in the 1940's and 50's. In English, called Gatherers of the Sound of Love of Life. Provided members with funeral expenses. Contributed to charitable institutions.

Minutes, 1949-60; financial records, 1959-70.

274. Kodima Benevolent Society, Inc.
Records, 1935-1973, 10" (RG 864)

Incorporated in 1929 and dissolved in 1973. Activities included the establishment of a ladies auxiliary.

Minutes, 1959-73; financial records, 1940's-70's; membership records, 1966-70; correspondence, 1950's-70's; burial permits, 1935-71; seal; stamp.

275. Lady McKinley Benevolent Society
Records, 1907, 1936-1972, 2½" (RG 952)

Organized in 1901. Also known as Lady McKinley Lodge. Dissolved 1972.

Financial records; cemetery permits; correspondence; miscellaneous.

276. Leah Benevolent Society
Records, 1924-1967, 7½" (RG 929)

A women's society established in the 1880's to provide sick benefits, death benefits, burial for members. Dissolved after 1967.

Financial records, 1920's-50's; cemetery permits.

277. Loyal American Lodge No. 402, Independent Order of Odd Fellows
Records, 1925-1970, 8″ (RG 871)

Founded in 1925 as a fraternal lodge of the I.O.O.F. Provided mutual aid and social benefits for members. Established cemetery, distress, sick benefit committees. Supported various philanthropies.

By-laws; minutes, 1925-28, 1940-44; financial records, 1946-48, 1953-70; correspondence, 1930's-40's.

278. Loyal Benevolent Society, Inc.
Records, 1886-1969, 1′3″ (RG 900)

Established in 1886 as the Hirsch Liska Lodge No. 66, Order Brith Abraham. Also known as the Hirsch Liska Sick and Benevolent Society. Subsequently incorporated as an independent mutual-aid association.

By-laws; minutes of the Hirsch Liska Lodge, 1920-23 (German); of the Loyal B.S., 1923-49; financial records, 1940's-60's; materials pertaining to membership, 1886-1944 (German, English); correspondence; cemetery map; miscellaneous; voting box with black balls.

279. Max Rosh Beneficial Society of Harlem, Inc.
Records, 1903-1910, 1954-1971, 7½″ (RG 927)

Established in 1903. Named after Max Rosh, a founding member who served as the society's first treasurer. Dissolved 1971.

Minutes, 1903-10; financial records, 1954-70; materials pertaining to burial; correspondence.

280. Menorah Benevolent Society, Inc.
Records, 1919-1969, 5″ (RG 902)

Organized in 1905; incorporated in 1919 to provide medical assistance, burial endowments; social activities for members. Dissolved in the 1970's.

Minutes, 1919-60's; financial statements; membership applications; miscellaneous.

281. Moses Family Society, Inc.
Records, 1918-1979, 1′3″ (RG 839)

Established in 1910 by seven children of Moses Cohen, a Jewish immigrant from Srednik, Kovno province, Lithuania. Original purpose was to hold family get-togethers; establish a loan fund; provide death benefits. Current activities include charitable work, social functions, burial.

Constitution; minutes, 1961-77, including financial reports; financial records, 1950's-60's; membership records; correspondence; bulletins, 1938-76; anniversary journals; invitations; family trees; photographs; tape recording of reminiscences of society's history, 1979.

282. Mount Sinai Hebrew Mutual Benefit Society
Records, 1935-1976, 7½" (RG 956)

Founded and chartered in 1870 for the "promotion of friendship and sociability among its members," payment of sick and death benefits; burial. Dissolved 1976.

Constitution; minutes, 1953-67; financial records, 1935-66; bulletins; materials pertaining to burial.

283. Nathan Marcus Benevolent Society, Inc.
Records, 1931-1973, 1 folder (RG 1053)

A mutual aid society, founding date unknown. Dissolved in the 1970's.

Correspondence, 1954-73; cemetery agreements.

284. Nocoma Club, Inc.
Records, 1952-1975, 5" (RG 977)

Incorporated in 1905. Instituted a benevolent fund in 1965 to further philanthropy. Dissolved 1974.

Constitutional amendments and resolutions; minutes, 1967-74; financial records, 1967-74; burial records; meeting notices; correspondence; seal.

285. Philip Bernstein Sick Benefit Association, Inc.
Records, 1894, 1965, 1971-1975, 2½" (RG 925)

Organized in 1893 by 10 men attending the burial in Washington Cemetery, Brooklyn, of a friend, Philip Bernstein, a Rumanian immigrant. Incorporated in 1894. Established an old age fund to assist older members in paying dues, 1940. Dissolved 1975.

Certificate of incorporation, leather-bound, 1894; constitution; minutes, 1971-75; membership records; seal.

286. Progress Mutual Aid Society
Records, 1905-1964, 2'3½" (RG 1021)

Established in 1905. Was associated with a ladies auxiliary. Dissolved 1964.

Minutes, 1905-64; financial records, 1940's-60's; membership records, 1912-40, 1951-56; burial records; correspondence, materials pertaining to dissolution.

287. Rappaport Family Circle, Inc.
Records, 1952-1961, 1½" (RG 1076)

Organized in 1939 to promote closer relationships between descendents of Gershon Leibe and Bella Rappaport; to aid and assist each other and provide burial. Sponsored many social events.

Constitution; financial materials, 1954-61; correspondence; banner.

288. Selective Brothers of Israel, Inc.
Records, 1928-1963, 7½" (RG 928)

Founding date unknown. Collected head tax from members to pay for endowments.

Constitutional amendments; minutes, 1936-51; financial records, 1940's-50's; materials pertaining to burial; correspondence.

289. Shonberg (Shoenberg) Family Aid Society
Records, 1916-1969, 2½" (RG 1078)

Organized in 1912 and incorporated in 1915 to strengthen family ties; materially and financially assist sick and needy members. Membership open to Shonberg direct descendents and spouses. Founders originated from the Warsaw area.

Certificate of incorporation; constitution; minutes, 1936-58; miscellaneous, 1916-69.

New Year's card sent by the lines-hatsedek *(hospital committee),* moyshev-zkeynim *(old age home) and* hakhnoses-orkhim *(shelter for guests or wanderers) in Radzivilov to the society in New York. (Donated by the Radziviller-Woliner Benevolent Association)*

290. Tremont Benevolent Society, Inc.
Records, 1943, 1957-1975, 5" (RG 939)

Founded in 1910 as the Tremont Lodge No. 386, Independent Order Brith Abraham. Later changed name to Tremont Benevolent Society, Inc. Provided mutual aid, charitable, social, burial functions. Maintained ties with I.O.B.A.; merged funds of Lodge No. 386 with its own in 1966.

Constitutions; minutes, 1965-74; financial records, 1957-75; seal.

291. True Brethren Benevolent Association
Records, 1919-1975, 12½" (RG 924)

Founded in 1909 as a benevolent society with no European regional or home town base. Members are mostly American born.

Legal documents; minutes, 1930's-40's; financial records, 1940's-70's; membership applications; burial permits; correspondence.

292. United Family of Moses Joseph
Records, 1911-1970, 8" (RG 1067)

Organized in 1911 as a family benevolent society. Maintained a loan fund; provided sick and death benefits. Associated with a ladies auxiliary and a junior league.

Minutes, 1911-30, 1933-57; financial records, 1925-50's, 1970; meeting announcements; society papers.

293. United Jewish Organizations (Fareynikte Yidishe Organizatsiyes)
Records, 1933-1937, 2' 6" (RG 259)

Organized in 1934 as an independent association of Jewish *landsmanshaftn*, fraternal, and benevolent societies. Aimed to "help the *landsmanshaftn* and societies to help themselves through cooperative planning and joint action." Dissolved 1937.

Financial records; appointment and address books; administrative records, including minutes, bulletins; materials pertaining to conferences, including principles of organization, banquets, celebrations; guest and membership lists; speeches; skits; souvenir journals; materials pertaining to cultural programming; correspondence with over 150 societies; memoranda; newspaper clippings; miscellaneous, including the annual report of the American Jewish Joint Distribution Committee, part II, 1936.

294. United Sons of Israel, Inc.
Records, 1940-1979, 8" (RG 846)

Established in 1929 as the United Artists Fraternity, a fraternal organization of men and women in the arts. Reestablished in 1940 as the United Sons of Israel of the Bronx, Inc., and in 1953 as the United Sons of Israel, Inc. Affiliated with the Ladies Auxiliary of the United Sons of Israel, Inc.

Certificate of incorporation, United Sons of Israel, Inc., 1953; constitution, United Sons of Israel of the Bronx, Inc.; minutes, 1940-57; membership records; materials relating to burial; bulletins; materials relating to the Ladies Auxiliary.

295. Unity Friendship League, Inc. and/or Moses Mendelsohn Lodge No. 91, Independent Order Brith Abraham
Records, 1920-1974, 1' 8 " (RG 931)

Established in 1893 as the Moses Mendelsohn Lodge No. 91, I.O.B.A. Changed name to Unity Friendship League, Inc., while maintaining relationship with the Grand Lodge I.O.B.A. for those members still wishing to be affiliated with that fraternal order.

Constitution, Unity Friendship League; minutes, Moses Mendelsohn Lodge, 1920-26 (German, English), 1926-33 (English); financial records, 1956-74; membership records; publications; materials pertaining to burial; correspondence, 1956-74; materials pertaining to dissolution; materials relating to Brith Abraham; stamp, Mendelsohn Lodge.

Residents of Brisk holding matzes *for Passover holiday, purchased with funds sent by the United Brisker Relief, New York, 1921. (Donated by Jacob Finkelstein, United Brisker Relief)*

APPENDIX

APPENDIX I **Materials received after the completion of the *Landsmanshaftn* Project**

Appendix I alphabetically lists those societies and individuals which donated records to the YIVO Institute after the completion of the *Landsmanshaftn* Project in 1981. Where available, short organizational histories and descriptions of records are cited.

296. Chevra Bnei Shomrei Israel of Brownsville
Records, 1924-1970's, 15" (RG 1180)

Founded in 1924. Provided *gmiles-khesed* and *khevre-kedishe* services.

Minutes, 1924-1950's; ledgers; loan books; stamps; correspondence; photograph.

297. Congregation Tiferes Beth Jacob—Ezras Israel Anshei Bronx
Records, 1923-1950's, 3" (RG 1164)

Leather-bound, calligraphic *pinkes* of the *khevre-kedishe*, including minutes of the *khevre-kedishe*; record of plots, Kletzker Bruderlicher Unterstitzungs Ferein, 1923-43.

298. Covadlo, Walter J. (1902-   )
Papers, 1946-1981, 5" (RG 1162)

Former president of the Rypiner Benevolent Society, officer of the Dobrzyn-Rypiner Benevolent Association, member of the McKinley Lodge, active in fund raising for Israel.

Miscellaneous papers, 1940's to date, documenting his organizational activities for the Dobrzyn-Rypiner B.A.; Rypiner B.S.; Rypiner Relief Committee; Fraternal Division, United Jewish Appeal; Fraternal Division, State of Israel Bonds; Fraternal Division, Histadrut, and the National Ort League.

299. Erste Sandowa Wishner K.U.V.
Records, 1949-1980, 2½" (RG 1151)

Founded in 1919. Supported a small synagogue from 1919 to 1941. Ran dances, dinners, weekends in Lakewood and the Catskills for a membership of 75 families. Provided burial and other benefits. Dissolved.

Minutes; financial records (2 books); constitution.

300. Kalisher Landsmanshaft and Vicinity, Workmen's Circle Branch 361; Kalisher Non Partisan Relief Committee
Records, 1950's-1970's, (RG 1161)

Souvenir journals; Polish articles on Kalisz; minutes, 1960's-1970's; correspondence; invitations; flyers; photographs from pre and post WWII Poland; memorial book.

301. Onward Society
Records, 1913-1983, 1'10" (RG 1159)

Organized in 1912 as a club of American born young men to send a neighborhood boy with tuberculosis to Denver. Reformed in 1925 as part of the I.O.B.A. Established independent society in 1927. At its peak had 700-800 members with 10 committees. Provided sick and hospital benefits, social activities and burial. Active in WWII relief. Published the journal *Onward Spirit,* 1913-1983.

Minutes, 1940-1983; album of clippings from *Onward Spirit,* 1913-1948, editions, 1934-1983; printed matter; photographs; reports; publications; banner; trophy; altar cloth; plaque.

302. First Tlumaczer Benevolent Society
Records, 1916-1937, 7½" (RG 1172)

Minute book, 1916-1973; 3 ledgers.

303. Subject Collection: *Landsmanshaftn* (See Appendix II)
Records, 1905-1980, 13' (RG 123)

Materials pertaining to over 500 Jewish locality-based and non-locality based benevolent societies and federations in New York, other major American cities, and Israel. For a detailed listing, see appendix on page 83.

APPENDIX II Subject Collection: *Landsmanshaftn* (Entry 303, RG 123)

BOX 1 Adella Schweiger B.S., Inc.
Agudas Achim Aid Society
First Alexandrier Indep. Assn., Inc.
Amdurer B.A.
First American Benev. Assn. of Brooklyn, Inc.
Amschenover Indep. B.S.
Amstel B.A., Ind.
Anshei Sode Loven B.A. (Philadelphia)

Apter Fraternal Society, Inc.
Bakers Benevolent Assn. of Brownsville
United Baltic & Lithuanian Relief Federation
Baltic-Vitebsker Br. 33 I.W.O.
Baran Roumanian Ladies B.S.
Baranovker Woliner Ladies Relief (Philadelphia)
Baranowicher Farband of America, Inc.
New Baranowicher Br. 446 J.N.W.A.
Barsher Relief
Belchatower Landslayt
Belzer True Friends
Benderer Prog. Society, Inc.
Fraternal Order of Bendin-Sosnowicer
Benjamin Winter Br. 425, J.N.W.A.
Berdichever B.A. of Philadelphia
Berdichever Landslayt and Book Committee
Berdichever Prog. Society (Detroit)
Berditchever Kletsker Aid Society
First Bereg-Munkacser S.B.S.
Berezdiver-Woliner B.A. (Philadelphia)
Cong. Fannie Siegel Ind. Berlader Roumanian
First Berlader Roumanian B.A.

BOX 2

Bershader B.S.
Bershader Relief Committee
Bershader Book Committee
Erste Bershader Ladies K.U.V. (Newark)
Bershader Prog. Assn. (Philadelphia)
Bes Hamedresh Hagadol Agudas Achim Anshei Sfard
   of Coney Island, Inc.
Bialer Prog. Ladies Auxiliary
Bialystoker Book Committee
Bialystoker Center & Bikur Cholim Ladies Auxiliary
Bialystoker Center & Home for the Aged
Bialystoker Center & Bikur Cholim
Bialystoker-Rayoner Br. 88 W.C.
Bialystoker U.V. "Somech Noflim"
Club of Bialystoker Friends
Bialystok Jewish Historical Assn., Inc.
Bialystoker Synagogue
Bielotzerkover Br. 17 I.W.O.
United Bilgorayer Benevolent & Aid Society
First Bilizerker Wolyner B.S.
Bnai Eleazer, Inc.
Bnai Isaac Family Circle
Bnai Meyer Levit, Inc.
American Jewish Committee of Byelorussian Descent

BOX 3

Bobroisk B.A. (Philadelphia)
Indep. Bogopolier B.A. (Philadelphia)
First Bolechower S.B.A.
Borisov & Vicinity Relief Committee
Boslover B.A.
Brailover Prog. B.A. of Philadelphia
Brainsker Brothers Aid Assn.
Chebra Anshei Brainsk Sheves Achim
Brainsker Y.M.B.A.
Brestitshker Landslayt
Brezover Benev. Brotherhood & Religious Division,
    Cong. Anshe Brezow
First Brezower Bruck S.B.S.
Britchever Prog. Society
Chevra Ohev Shalom Anshei Bukaczowce
Adjutoral Bukarester Handwerker Cong.
Bukowinaer Center
Burstyner Chevra Linas Hazedek Anshei Galizia
Central Committee of Patronati
Chabner Bazarer Society, Inc.
Chechanov-Mlaver Patronat in New York
Chelmer Landslayt
Cherkasser Prog. Ladies Auxiliary
First Chernelitzer S.B.A.
Chernigover B.A.
Chernowitz Podolier Aid Assn.
Chevra Kadisha—The Holy Society of the City of New York
Chevra Mishnayos of East New York
Chevra Ohav Shalom Nusach HaAri of Brooklyn
Association of Former Residents of China
First Chodorower Society
Indep. Chodorower Y.M.B.A.
Chotiner Hospital Moshev Zkenim Relief
Chotiner Yugend Br. 271 W.C.
Chudnover Indep. B.S.
Chvonicker Indep. Aid Assn.
Chvonicker Ladies Club
Committee of Jewish Landsmanshaftn and Societies—United
    Committee of Jewish Societies and Landsmanshaft Federations
Cong. Taharas Hakoidesh Aid Society, Inc.
Constantiner Preiaslover Lodge 245 Ind. Order Brith Sholem
Council of Fraternal and Benevolent Organizations for the
    Support of Jewish Philanthropic Societies of N.Y.C.
Council of Jewish Fraternal Federations

BOX 4

New Cracow Friendship Society, Inc.
Cuban-David Bliss Br. 422 Farband L.Z.O.
Czortkower Congregation (Society of Rabbi Shapiro)
Denburger B.A. (Philadelphia)
Devenishker Ladies Auxiliary
Dinewitz Podolier U.V. (Philadelphia)

Cong. Bnei Rappaport Anshei Dombrowa
Indep. Drobniner B.S. of New York
Drohobyczer Landslayt
Drushkopoler Wohliner B.A. Society (Philadelphia)
Dvinsker Bund Br. 75 W.C.
Women's Mutual Aid Society of Ekaterinoslav
Ezra B.S.
Family B.S.
Fannie Abrams Indep. B.S., Inc.
Free Sons of Israel
Chevra Bnai Yechiel Anshei Frystik
Galatzer Ladies Auxiliary
Federation of Galician and Bucovinian Jews of America
United Galician Jews of America
United Galil Aid Soiciety, Inc.

BOX 5

Glinianer Y.M.B.A., Inc.
Cong. Anshei Gliniany
Goniondzer-Trestiner Young Friends
Goniondzer Relief Committee
First Indep. Gostyniner B.A. War Relief Committee
Greater City B.A., Inc.
Indep. Greidinger Podolier B.A.
First Haliczer B.A.
Hebrew Orphan Asylum Assn.
Homler Brothers Society
Homler Credit Union
Ladies Auxiliary of the Homler Shul Ahavas Chesed
Cong. Anshei Horodetz
Horodischer Brothers B.A.
Horodler Relief Committee
Hoschter Society
Howard Friends League, Inc.
United Hrubieshower Relief
Chevra Kadisha Reim Ahuvim M'Hrubieshow Anshei Poylin
American Hungarian Jewish Federation
Independent Order Bnai Brith
Independent Order Brith Abraham
Independent Order Brith Sholom
Independent Order Sons of Benjamin

BOX 6

Israel Cantor Family Society
Ivier Relief
First Izbitzer Relief Committee
Jaroslauer Congregation K.U.V.
Kalarasher Bessarabier Prog. Assn.
First Kalnibloder B.S., Inc.
Indep. Kalushiner B.A.
Indep. Kaluszer S.B.S.
Indep. Kamenetz Podolier Society, Inc.
Kartuz-Berezer Social & B.A.

Indep. Keidenover B.A., Inc. of Brooklyn
Kiblicher Society
Kiever-Homler Congregation Society, Inc.
Kiever Indep. B.A. of Brooklyn
Kings County Prog. B.S., Inc.
Indep. Kisheneff B.S.
Kishinever Relief and Charity Society
Kishinever Home for the Aged
Kishinever Talmud Torah, Inc.
Prog. Kitaigoroder Podolier B.S.

BOX 7

Kletsker Memorial Book
Indep. Kletzker Brotherly Aid Assn.
First Klewaner B.A.
Kobriner Br. 250 Farband L.Z.O.
Kobriner Ladies Benevolent Auxiliary
First Komarover B.S.
Ladies & Men's Society of Konin and Surrounding Towns
Konopter Y.M.B.A.
Old Konstantiner Landslayt
First Koretzer S.B.S. of New York
Korsoner Verein of Philadelphia, Ladies Auxiliary
Indep. Korwer Prog. Y.M.B.S., Inc.
Kovler Voliner Y.M.B.A.
Committee for the Jewish Industrial Center in Kovno
Kozienietzer Aid Society
Krakinover B.A.
Chevra Bnai Arya Anshai Krasnapolie
Kremenitz-Ouiezd Relief Committee (Chicago)
First Krementshuger B.A.
Kultchiner Relief Committee
First Kunever Voliner Aid Society, Inc.
Kurlander Y.M. Mutual A.S.
Kuzminer Voliner Young Friends Society
Memorial Committee of Lachowicze & Vicinity
First Ladziner Aid Society
First Lanowitzer Woliner Y.M.B.A.
Latvian Jews
Assn. of Latvian and Estonian Jews in Israel
Lipkaner Israel Refuge Fund, Inc.
Lipner Y.M.B.S., Inc.
Lipovitzer Aid Society
Lissianker Prog. Assn.

BOX 8

Lithuanian Landslayt
Lithuanian Jewish Youth
American Federation for Lithuanian Jews
Farband of Lithuanian Jews
Jewish-Lithuanian Cultural Society "Lite," Inc.
Jewish Lithuanian Org. of America, Inc.
United Lithuanian Jews of America

Women's Aid Society of Lithuanian Jews, Inc.
Lodzer Br. 324 W.C.
Lodzer Lodge No. 609 Knights of Pythias
Ghetto Lodz Memorial Synagogue
Indep. Lodzer Y.M. (N.J.)
Louis D. Brandeis B.S.
Lowitcher Yisker Book Committee
K'hal Adat Jeshurun with Anshei Lubitz
Lubliner Ehrlich Br. 392 W.C. and Ladies Club
United Lubliner Relief
Pinkas Luboml Aid Committee, Inc.
Lukashivker Landslayt—B.A. of Faithful Friends, Inc.
Lukower Br. 153, I.W.O.
Louis Levine/Royal Lodge No. 198 Brith Sholom
Erste Magierower K.U.V.
Maimonides B.S.
Jewish Majdaner Verein
First Maravcher Podoler Aid Society
Mariampoler Aid Society (Chicago)
Federated Marmaros Jews of America
First Marmaros Y.M.A.S., Inc.
Cong. Volin Anshei Matziv
Mazirer & Vicinity Relief Committee of Philadelphia and
    Ladies Auxiliary (with the United Brahiner Relief of Phil.)
Medgibosh Prog. Solidarity Society
Meicheter Brotherly Aid Assn.
Ershter Melitopol Assn.
Mendelsohn B.S.
Meritzer Relief Assn.

BOX 9

Meseritzer Ladies Aid Society of Greater New York
Meshbisher U.V.
Mezhirover Brotherly B.S.
Minsk Chronicle Publication Committee
Minsker Indep. B.A.
Minsker Prog. Br. 99 W.C.
Bronx Relief Committee for Minsk & Vicinity
United Minkowitz-Podolier Relief
Indep. Mlaver K.U.V.
Mlaver Pinkes Committee
United Mlaver Relief Committee
Moghilev-Podolsk Fellowship
United Moghilev Podolier and Otiker Relief
Cong. Chevra Molodetchno & Ladies Auxiliary
Morris Mendelson Y.M.B.S.
Gross Moster S.B.A.
First Gross Moster Ladies Society
Mozirer Aid Society
Musher and Baranowitcher B.A.
Narovler Aid Society
Alexander Harkavy Navaridker Relief Committee
Prog. Brethren of Neshwiss

Newmark Y.M.B.A
Niagara Society, Inc.
First Nickolayever S.B.A.

BOX 10

Novoselitzer Prog. Br. 498, W.C.
Indep. Nowe-Dworer B.A.
First Novo-Ushitzer B.S.
Nowo-Radomsker United Relief Committee
Nowoselitzer Ladies S.B.S., Inc.
Odessa Prog. Aid Society
Odessa Mutual Relief Assn.
Odessa United Relief
Odesser Y.M.P.A. (Philadelphia)
Oshmaner & Trab Assn.
Chevra Bikur Cholim Bnai Abraham Anshei Ostreich D'Harlem
Ostrer Maharsho Lodge 160 Ind. Order Brith Sholom
  (Philadelphia)
Ostrer Marsho Ladies Auxiliary (Philadelphia)
First Ostropolier Prog. Aid Assn. (Philadelphia)
United Ostrover Relief Committee
Combined Ostrovtzer Committee (Philadelphia)
Ladies Auxiliary, Ostrovtzer Indep. Mutual Society (Philadelphia)
Ostrow-Mazowieck Memorial Journal
First Ostrower S.B.S.
Otick Mohilever Y.M.B.A.
Indep. Otik Mohiliv B.A. (Philadelphia)
Pereyaslov Prog. Assn. (N.J.)
Pestchonker Prog. B.A. of Philadelphia
Petrikower Y.M.B.A.
Indep. Petrikower Aid Society
First Piaterer Roumanian S.B.S.
Pietrykower Landslayt
Pilover Landslayt
First Pilzer B.S.
Erhste Pinchover U.V.
Pinsker Br. 210 W.C.
Pinsker Relief Committee for the Pinsker Jewish War Sufferers
Joint Pinsker Relief Committee
Pinsker Aid Society (Los Angeles)
Pinsker Memorial Book (3 volumes, Box 11)
Piotrkow & Vicinity Society, Inc.
Pitchaever-Voliner B.A.
First Piusker B.A., Inc.
Poloner Prog. Ladies Auxiliary
First Poltaver Brotherly Aid Society

BOX 11

Pinsker Memorial Book (3 volumes)

Women's Aid Society of Lithuanian Jews, Inc.
Lodzer Br. 324 W.C.
Lodzer Lodge No. 609 Knights of Pythias
Ghetto Lodz Memorial Synagogue
Indep. Lodzer Y.M. (N.J.)
Louis D. Brandeis B.S.
Lowitcher Yisker Book Committee
K'hal Adat Jeshurun with Anshei Lubitz
Lubliner Ehrlich Br. 392 W.C. and Ladies Club
United Lubliner Relief
Pinkas Luboml Aid Committee, Inc.
Lukashivker Landslayt—B.A. of Faithful Friends, Inc.
Lukower Br. 153, I.W.O.
Louis Levine/Royal Lodge No. 198 Brith Sholom
Erste Magierower K.U.V.
Maimonides B.S.
Jewish Majdaner Verein
First Maravcher Podoler Aid Society
Mariampoler Aid Society (Chicago)
Federated Marmaros Jews of America
First Marmaros Y.M.A.S., Inc.
Cong. Volin Anshei Matziv
Mazirer & Vicinity Relief Committee of Philadelphia and Ladies Auxiliary (with the United Brahiner Relief of Phil.)
Medgibosh Prog. Solidarity Society
Meicheter Brotherly Aid Assn.
Ershter Melitopol Assn.
Mendelsohn B.S.
Meritzer Relief Assn.

BOX 9

Meseritzer Ladies Aid Society of Greater New York
Meshbisher U.V.
Mezhirover Brotherly B.S.
Minsk Chronicle Publication Committee
Minsker Indep. B.A.
Minsker Prog. Br. 99 W.C.
Bronx Relief Committee for Minsk & Vicinity
United Minkowitz-Podolier Relief
Indep. Mlaver K.U.V.
Mlaver Pinkes Committee
United Mlaver Relief Committee
Moghilev-Podolsk Fellowship
United Moghilev Podolier and Otiker Relief
Cong. Chevra Molodetchno & Ladies Auxiliary
Morris Mendelson Y.M.B.S.
Gross Moster S.B.A.
First Gross Moster Ladies Society
Mozirer Aid Society
Musher and Baranowitcher B.A.
Narovler Aid Society
Alexander Harkavy Navaridker Relief Committee
Prog. Brethren of Neshwiss

Newmark Y.M.B.A
Niagara Society, Inc.
First Nickolayever S.B.A.

BOX 10

Novoselitzer Prog. Br. 498, W.C.
Indep. Nowe-Dworer B.A.
First Novo-Ushitzer B.S.
Nowo-Radomsker United Relief Committee
Nowoselitzer Ladies S.B.S., Inc.
Odessa Prog. Aid Society
Odessa Mutual Relief Assn.
Odessa United Relief
Odesser Y.M.P.A. (Philadelphia)
Oshmaner & Trab Assn.
Chevra Bikur Cholim Bnai Abraham Anshei Ostreich D'Harlem
Ostrer Maharsho Lodge 160 Ind. Order Brith Sholom
 (Philadelphia)
Ostrer Marsho Ladies Auxiliary (Philadelphia)
First Ostropolier Prog. Aid Assn. (Philadelphia)
United Ostrover Relief Committee
Combined Ostrovtzer Committee (Philadelphia)
Ladies Auxiliary, Ostrovtzer Indep. Mutual Society (Philadelphia)
Ostrow-Mazowieck Memorial Journal
First Ostrower S.B.S.
Otick Mohilever Y.M.B.A.
Indep. Otik Mohiliv B.A. (Philadelphia)
Pereyaslov Prog. Assn. (N.J.)
Pestchonker Prog. B.A. of Philadelphia
Petrikower Y.M.B.A.
Indep. Petrikower Aid Society
First Piaterer Roumanian S.B.S.
Pietrykower Landslayt
Pilover Landslayt
First Pilzer B.S.
Erhste Pinchover U.V.
Pinsker Br. 210 W.C.
Pinsker Relief Committee for the Pinsker Jewish War Sufferers
Joint Pinsker Relief Committee
Pinsker Aid Society (Los Angeles)
Pinsker Memorial Book (3 volumes, Box 11)
Piotrkow & Vicinity Society, Inc.
Pitchaever-Voliner B.A.
First Piusker B.A., Inc.
Poloner Prog. Ladies Auxiliary
First Poltaver Brotherly Aid Society

BOX 11

Pinsker Memorial Book (3 volumes)

OBJECTS AND OVERSIZED MATERIALS
Seals, gavels, banners, realia, etc.

Society Name
Agudas Achim Aid Society
Chevra Ayin Yakub Kenesis Israel, Inc.
Chevra Kadishe Anshei Chodorow
Chevre Linas Hatsedek Anshei Lublin
Chrzanower Y.M.A.
CLM
Cong. Bnei Aharon Anshei Wilkomir
Employees of Charles Brodsky
Ezra B.S.
First Alexandria Indep. Assn., Inc.
First Congregation of Israel People of Tarler
First Independent Junkower Aid Society
First Kalischer Y.M.B.S.
First Roumanian American Congregation
First Werenczanker Bucowinaer K.U.V.
Goverover Y.M.B.A.
Kiever Independent
Kings County Prog. B.S., Inc.
Krasnopoler Y.M. Br. 623 W.C.
Ladzin family photo (Dashefsky family)
Landsleit newspaper
Lodge costumes, miscellaneous
Morris Greif Lodge No. 33
Pannonia Rebekah Lodge No. 130, I.O.O.F.
Plotzker Memorial
Progressive Sisters of Neshwiss
Rawa Mazowietsk Yisker Certificate
Rutger Benevolent Society
Superior Lodge No. 401, I.O.O.F.
Tolchiner-Mlaver Society
United Galician Jews
United Jewish Appeal, Council of Organizations
Woolwich materials on Ostre and Priluki

An enameled souvenir button.

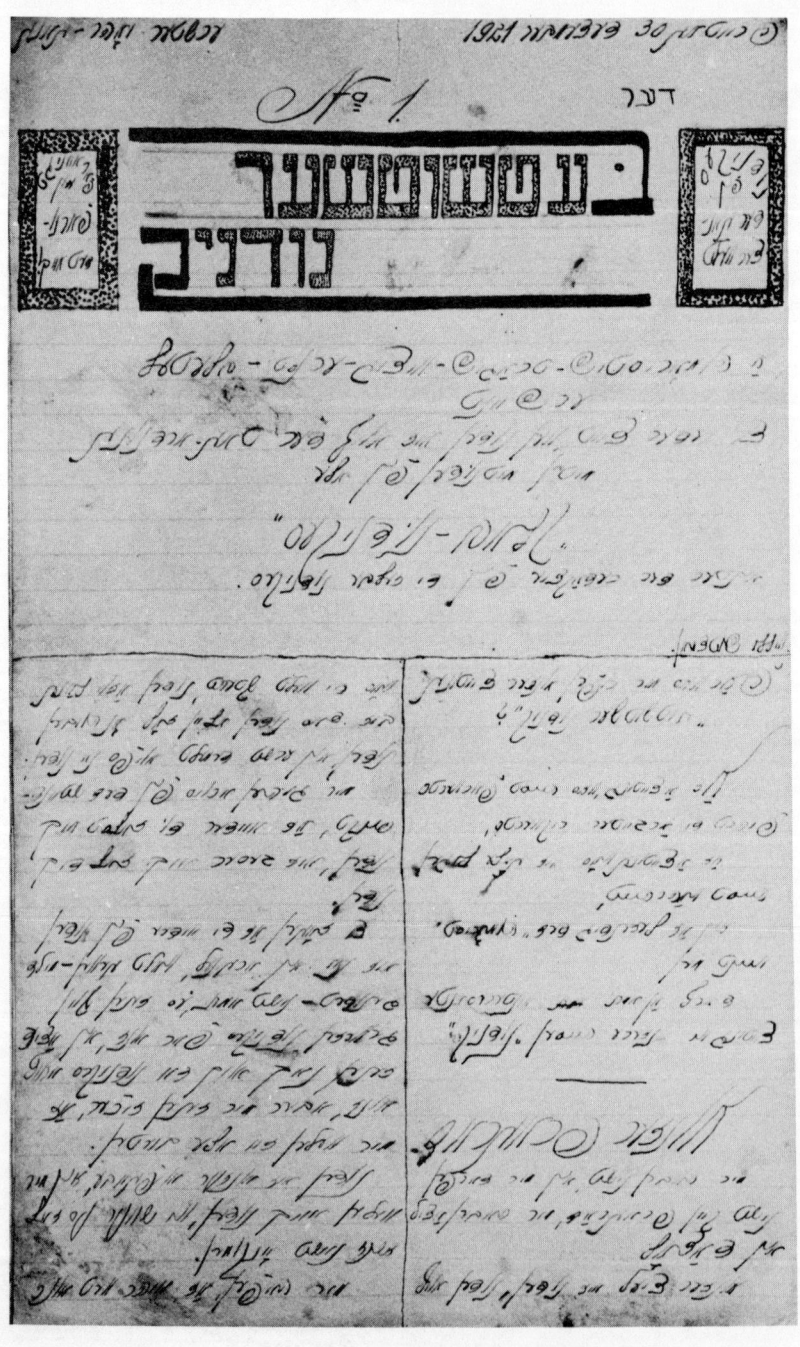

Handwritten newspaper, The Betschutsher Nudnik: *"a humorous, tragic, witty, serious newspaper appears whenever 'nudyen' is on the agenda,"* 1921. (Donated by the Buczacz-American Benevolent Sick and Aid Society)

BOX 12

Ponevezer Prog. Y.M.B.A.
United Brethren of Ponivesh Assn.
Prager Warschauer Y.M.A.S.
First Prailer S.B.A.
Prener Bruderlicher U.V.
United Priluker Relief Society
Provident S.B.S.
Prushin-Shershow B.A. (Philadelphia)
Indep. Prushnitzer S.B.S.
Pruzaner Br. 244 W.C.
United Pruzaner & Vicinity Relief Committee
Przemyslaner Relief Societies and Brodyer Societies
United Przemyslaner Matzoh and Talmud Torah Fund
Congregation Puchowitzer
Pultusker Prog. Society
Pultusker R.Y. Br. 494 W.C.
Rachower Polish Jewish Federation
United Rachover Relief
Radautz Roumanian B.S. and Relief Committee
Indep. Radiviler Voliner B.A. (Philadelphia)
Indep. Radom Aid Assn.
Radomysler-Chernichover Br. 543 W.C.
Radomysler Y.M.B.A. No. 1
United Radomysler Relief
First Radymnoer Congregation Bnai Mordechai Menachem
Rakishker Society (So. Africa)
Rakower Ladies Club
Rashkower Prog. Assn. (Philadelphia)
Chevre Sheveth Achim Anshei Ratchantz
Riga Relief
Erster Romaner K.U.V. Young Folks League
Rossover-Krilivitzer B.A. (Philadelphia) and Ladies Auxiliary

BOX 13

Heart of Roumanian Y.M.B.A., Inc.
Committee of Roumanian Jews
Indep. Rovner B.A. Philadelphia
Rozniatower Yisker Book
Rubzevitzer Y.M.B.A.
Rumanian Memorial Committee
Rutker Landslayt
Ryki Yisker Book
Rymanower Y.M.B.A.
Rzeszower Young Men's Social B.S.

BOX 14

Prog. Schmilowitzer Young Friends
United Schmilewitzer Relief Committee
Schumiacher-Odesser Br. 123 J.N.W.A.
Schwerzner B.A.
First Indep. Securaner Relief B.A.
First Securaner Relief

Selzer B.A.
Committee of Semiatycher Yiskor Book of New York
Semionovker B.S., Inc.
Shadover Relief Society of Greater New York
Shargarad Podolier K.U.V.
Sharograder Prog. B.A. (Philadelphia)
Shater Prog. Relief Committee of Shater Prog. B.A.
Shatover Podolier Indep. Society
Shedletzer Landslayt
Cong. Anshe Shepetovka Volin (Boston)
First Shepetovker Y.M.A.
Shepetovker B.A. (Philadelphia)
First Shpoler B.S.
Shrentzker B.A.
Federation of Shavler & Vicinity
Simferapol Relief and Vicinity
Skalater Prog. Y.F.B.A.
Skarzshisker Landslayt
Skurnick Family Circle
Slominker Landsleit of Israel
Indep. Slonimer B.S.
Chevra Kadusha Anshei Sochaczow
Chevre Sokal-Belz
Sokolifker B.A. (Philadelphia)
Sokolifker Ladies Auxiliary (Philadelphia)
Sokolover Jubilee Book Committee
First Solotwiner S.B.S.
Soroker Teleneshter Bessarabia S.B.A. (Philadelphia)
Indep. Stabzer B.A.
Stashover B.A. (Michigan)
First Stavishter B.A.
Stavisker Y.M.B.A.
Stchedriner B.S., Inc.
First Stepiner Ladies Auxiliary
Indep. Stepnitzer B.A. (Philadelphia)
Indep. Stryjer B.S.
United Stryjer Y.M.B.A.
Cong. Anshei Stuchin and Grayewo
Stuchiner Y.M.B.A.
Sudilkov-Shepetowka Relief Society (Chicago)
Cong. Anshei Smorgon Bnei Chaim Abraham

BOX 15

Cong. Mishkan Israel Anshe Suwalker
Indep. Suwalker B.A.
Swirer Social & Aid Society
Szatmar & Vicinity Hungarian S.B.S.
First Tarler Congregation
T.D. (Tarnobrzeg Dzikow) Y.M.A.
First Tarnower K.U.V.

BOX 16

Telechaner-Swentevolier S.B.S
Teplicker B.A.
First Tepliker Benev. Congregation Society
Ternovker Relief
Titshiner Relief Committee
Tlumaczer Y.F. Br. 616 W.C.
Tomashover Yisker Book
Chebra Bnai Tomashow K.U.V.
Tomashover Relief Committee
Tomashover Yizkor Book Committee
Trestiner Ladies Auxiliary
Tultshiner Landslayt
Turover Aid Society (Michigan)
Federation of Ukrainian Jews (in America)
Union of Jews of Ukrainian Descent, Inc.
Ulanower Congregation and Umgegend
Umaner Young Friends Club
Adath Israel Anshei Ungarn, Inc. (Hungary)
United Committee of Jewish Societies and Landsmanshaft Federations
United Hebrew Community (Adath Israel)
Ustila, Ludmir, and Suburbs Memorial Committee

BOX 17

Utianer Landslayt
Vilkija-Kweskin Family
United Taomidei Visheve
Vitebsker Book Committee
Vladower Vladowker Y.M.B.A.
Vlotzlawker Memorial Book Committee
Indep. Voliner Aid Society
Volkovinitzer-Podolier B.A. (Philadelphia)
Volper Y.M.S., Inc.
Chevra Ahavas Achim Anshei Volp U'Most
Voronover Y.M.B.A.
First Waroshilovker B.A.
Warschauer Brotherhood of New York
Warschauer Relief
Warschauer Y.F.B.S. of Brownsville
Warschauer Y.M.B.A.
Warshawer Social Friends
Harlem Indep. Warschauer Society
Ezras Achim Anshe Widze
Wilkemira Y.M.B.A.
Cong. Anshe Wilkomir
Indep. Winnitzer Lodge. No. 274 I.O.B.A. (Philadelphia)
Winnitzer Ladies Auxiliary (Philadelphia)
United Winnitzer Y.M.B.A.
Wishkover B.S.
Wishnewitz Yisker Book

BOX 18

United Relief Committee of Wisoke Mazowietzk
Wisoko-Litovsker B.U.V.
Wisoko-Litovsker United Relief
Erste Wogdislauer U.V.
Wolbromer Landslayt
Wolkowinitzer-Podolier Aid Society & Ladies Group
Wolkowisker Y.M.B.A.
Wolochisker B.A.
Wolochisker Relief Committee
Wolochisker Ladies Auxiliary
Yampoler B.A. of Philadelphia
Yaniv-Lubelsky Congregation
Yarmolinitzer B.S.
United Yarmolinitzer Relief
First Yompoler Podoler B.S.
First Yedinitzer Relief Org., Inc.
Yosser Society
Association of Yugoslav Jews in the U.S., Inc.
Yunover Y.M.B.A.
Erste Zabner Ladies Auxiliary
Chevra Bnai Jacob Yitzhak Anshei Zabne
Chevra Bnai Eliyahu Anshei Zager
Zaglembie-Volbrom Farband
Erste Zaloshiner Chevra Anshei Bnei Achim
Zamostcher Relief Committee
Zamoscher Yisker Book Committee (Argentina)
Friends of Zamosch (Philadelphia)
Zamoscher B.A. (Philadelphia)
Zamoscha Prog. Y.M.B.S. (Philadelphia)
Zamoscher Prog. Y.M. Br. 375 W.C.

BOX 19

Zaromber P.Y.F.B.A.
Zaslaver Relief Committee (Boston)
Zawiercer Prog. B.A.
First Zbarazer Relief Society, Inc.
Cong. Anshei Zembrove
Zembrover B.A., Inc.
Zerdover Educational Society Br. 301 W.C.
Zitomirer B.A. (Philadelphia)
Zloczower Relief Verband of America
Cong. Machzikei Hadas Anshei Zloczow
First Zloczower S.B.A.
First Zlotnicker S.B.S.
First Zolkiewer Ladies S.B.S.
Chevra Bikur Cholim Anshei Zuromin
Zvhiler Lodge No. 594 I.O.B.A.
Zwenigorodker B.A. (Philadelphia)
Zychliner Relief Committee of New York
Zychliner Y.M.B.S.

APPENDIX III Locations of Jewish Cemeteries in New York City and Environs

Burial in a society plot was a benefit offered by most *landsmanshaftn*. The following are the names and locations of Jewish burial grounds where these plots are located.

Acacia Cemetery
83-84 Liberty Avenue
Ozone Park, NY

Baron Hirsch Cemetery
1126 Richmond Avenue
Staten Island, NY

Bayside Cemetery
Ozone Park, NY

Beth David Cemetery
(Elmont Cemetery, Inc.)
Elmont, NY

Beth-El Cemeteries
(composed of Union Field, Machpelah and New Union Fields)
Cypress Hills Street
Ridgewood, NY

Beth-El Cemetery
Forest Avenue
Westwood, NJ

Beth Israel Memorial Park
on Route 1
Woodridge, NJ

Beth Moses Cemetery
Wellwood Avenue
Pinelawn (Suffolk County)
L.I., NY

Beth Olam Fields Cemetery
Brooklyn, NY

Cedar Park Cemetery
Westwood, NJ 07675

Cypress Hills Cemetery
Jamaica Avenue
Brooklyn, NY

Floral Park Cemetery
(formerly Degel Yehudo)
Rhode Hall Road
Monmouth Junction, NJ

King David Cemetery
Adams Corners
Putnam Valley, NY

King Solomon Memorial Park
Clifton, NJ

Knollwood Park Cemetery
Cooper and Cypress Avenues
Brooklyn, NY

Linden Hill Cemetery of Central Synagogue
5222 Metropolitan Avenue
Ridgewood, NY

Machpelah Cemetery Association
82-30 Cypress Hills Street
Flushing, NY

Maimonides Brooklyn Cemetery
Jamaica and Lincoln Avenues
Brooklyn, NY

Maimonides Elmont Cemetery
Elmont Road
Elmont, NY

Mokom Sholom Cemetery, Inc.
Ozone Park, NY 11417

Montefiore Cemetery
Springfield Blvd.
St. Albans, NY

Mount Ararat Cemetery
Babylon Road
Farmingdale, NY

Mount Carmel Cemetery
Cypress Hills Street &
Cypress Avenue
Glendale, NY

Mount Eden Cemetery
Commerce Street
Valhalla, NY

Mount Golda Cemetery
500 Old Country Road
Huntington Station, NY

Mount Hebron
Long Island Expressway &
College Point Blvd.
Flushing, NY

Mount Hope Cemetery
Saw Mill River Road
Hastings-on-Hudson, NY

Mount Hope Cemetery
Jamaica Avenue and
Nicholas Avenue
Brooklyn, NY

Mount Judah Cemetery
Cypress Avenue
Ridgewood, NY

**Mount Lebanon Cemetery
Association**
Iselin, NJ

Mount Lebanon Cemetery
7800 Myrtle Avenue
Glendale, NY

Mount Moriah Cemetery
Fairview, NJ

Mount Neboh Cemetery
82-07 Cypress Hills Street
Glendale, NY

**Mount Pleasant Westchester
Cemetery Corp.**
Hawthorne, NY

Mount Washington Cemetery
Coram, NY

Mount Zion Cemetery
Maspeth, NY

New Montefiore Cemetery
Wellwood Avenue
Pinelawn, NY

New Mount Carmel
Cypress Hill Street and
Cooper Avenue
Brooklyn, NY

New Mount Zion
Orient Way and Route 17
Lyndhurst, NJ

Patchogue Hebrew Cemetery
Buckley Avenue
Holtsville, NY

Riverside Cemetery
Rochelle Park, NJ

Salem Fields Cemetery
775 Jamaica Avenue
Brooklyn, NY

**Sanctuary of Abraham
and Sarah**
Paramus, NJ

Sharon Gardens
Valhalla, NY

Temple Israel Cemetery
Saw Mill River Road
Hastings-on-Hudson, NY

United Hebrew Cemetery, Inc.
122 Arthur Kill Road
Staten Island, NY

Union Field Cemetery
Cypress Avenue
Ridgewood, NY

Washington Cemetery of Deans
(See Floral Park Cemetery)
New Jersey

Washington Cemetery
McDonald Avenue and
Bay Parkway
Brooklyn, NY

Wellwood Cemetery
Wellwood Avenue
Pineland, NY

West Ridgelawn Cemetery
King Solomon Memorial
Park Section
Dwasline and Allwood Roads
Clifton, NJ

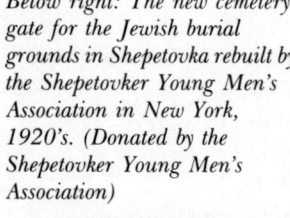

Below right: The new cemetery gate for the Jewish burial grounds in Shepetovka rebuilt by the Shepetovker Young Men's Association in New York, 1920's. (Donated by the Shepetovker Young Men's Association)

Below left: Cemetery gate and burial grounds of the Odesser Young Men of Harlem, S.B.A., Montefiore Cemetery, St. Albans, New York, 1985. (Photographer: Judith Helfand)

INDEX

Numbers in this index refer to entry, not page numbers.

Abraham Cohen B.S., Inc. 263
Agudas Achim Aid Society, 26
ALEXANDROVSK, 1
Alexandrowsker Relief, Inc., 1
American Council for Warsaw Jews, 242
American Federation for Aid to Polish Jews, 251
American Federation for Polish Jews, 170
ANIKSHCHYAI, 4
Anikster B.A., 4
Anikster Benev. Pischei Tshuvo Ass'n., Inc., 4
Anshe Lomza V'Gatch, 124
Antepoler Ladies Aux., 2
Antepoler Y.M.B.A., 2
Antepolier U.V., 3
ANTOPOL, 2, 3
ANYKSCIAI, 4
Associated Ben. Y.M. Inc., 243
Associated Lodzer Ladies Aid Soc., Inc., 121
AUSTILE, 234
BACAU, 5
Baltic Podolier Br. 277, I.W.O., 12
BARLAD, 6
BARYSH, BARYSZ, 7
Baryszer Y.M.B.A., Inc., 7
BELZ, 8
BEREZHANY, 9

BERLAD, 6
Bernstein, Philip, S.B.A., Inc., 285
BERSHAD, 10
Bershader B.S., Inc., 10
Bershader Book Committee, Inc., 10
BESHENKOVICHI, see also 38
BESSARABIA, 11, 12, 13, 14, 81
Bessarabian Federation of American Jews, Inc., 11, 14, 209, 210
Bessarabier Br. 302, I.W.O., 12
Bessarabier Podolier B.S., 12, 14
BEYTCH, 15
BIECZ, 15
BIELSK PODLASKI, 16
Bielsker Bruderlicher U.V., 16
BIRCZA, 17
Birczer Y.M.B.S., 17
Bistritz & Vicinity Ch. 33, Order Bnai Zion, 270
Bnai Rezitza Ass'n., Inc., 188
Bnai Zion (see also Order Bnai Zion), 99
BOBRUISK, BOBRUYSK, 18
BOGOPOL, 19
Bogopoler U.V., 19
BOLSHOVTSY, 20
BOLSZOWCE, 20
Boris Schatz B.S., Inc., 166
BORISLAV, see also 53
Borough of Brooklyn Lodge, 29
BORYSLAW, see also 53

BOTOSANI, BOTOSHANI, 21
Brainsker Bros. Aid Society, 22
BRANSK, 22
BRATISLAVA, 23
BRATSLAV, 24, 25
Braunstein, Dr., Society, 200
BREST 26
Breziner S.B.S., Inc., 31
BREZINY, 31
BRICENI, 27, 28
BRICHANY, 27, 28
BRISI NAD BUGIE, 26
BRISK, 26
Brisker & Vicinity Aid Society of Los Angeles, 26
Britchaner Bess. Relief Assn., 28
Brith Abraham (see Indep. Order Brith Abraham, Order Brith Abraham), 207
BRONX, 294, 297
BROOKLYN, 29, 30, 273
BROWNSVILLE, 240, 296
BRYANSK, 22
BRZEZANY, 9
BRZEZINY, 31
BUCHACH, 32
BUCHAREST, 33
BUCZACZ, 32
Buczacz-American B.S. & A.S., 32
BUDANOV, 34
BUDZANOW, 34
BURDUJENI, 35
BUSK, 36
Busker Bnai Brith S.B.A., 36
BUSKO, 36
CAUCASIA, 37
Caucasian B.S., Inc., 37
CAUCASUS, 37
Central Hungarian S.B. & Literary Society, 70
Ceres Union, 62
Chaim Hersch Weiss First Janover S.B.A., 74
Chasnick-Bieshenkowitzer Soc., 38
CHASHNIKI, 38
CHAUSSY, 39
Chebra Agudas Achim Anshei Radom, 181
Chechelnicker B.A. of Greater N.Y., Inc., 40
CHECHELNIK, 40
CHENCHIN, 82

Chenstochover Lodge No. 11, I.W.O., 46
Cherkasser-Smela B.A., Inc., 41
CHERKASSY, 41
CHERNOVTSY, 42
CHERVEN, 43
CHERVONOARMEISK, 44
Chevra, see also Khevre, Chebra
Chevra Ahavas Achim Anshei Korson, 98
Chevra Ahavath Achim B'nai Kolo, Inc., 89
Chevra Anshei Antepoler, 3
Chevra Bnei Israel Anshei Zurow, 261
Chevra Bnei Shomrei Israel of Brownsville, 296
Chevra Divrei Chaim, 93
Chevra Gomle Chesed Anshe Drohobych & Boryslaw, 53
Chevra Kadisha Beth Israel, 264
Chevra Mishnayos, 66
Chevra Oir Lashumaim Anshei Stopnitz, 216
Chevra Rodfey Tsedek Anshei Bolszowce, 20
CHMIELNIK, 45
Chmielniker S.B.S., 45
Chotiner-Bess. Emergency Club, 81
Circle of Buczaczer Friends, 32
Clay, Henry, Lodge No. 15, I.O.B.A., 166
Cohen, Abraham, B.S., Inc., 263
Committee for the Resettlement of Kielcer Jews, 82
Cong. Achei Grodno Vasapotkin & Chevra Mishnayos, 66
Cong. Adath Wolkowisk of Brownsville, 240
Cong. Agudas Achim Anshei Trembowla K.U.V., 225
Cong. Ahavath Achim Anshei Mohilev on Dnieper, 141
Cong. Ahavath Zedek Anshei Timkowitz, 227
Cong. Anshei Krashnik, 102
Cong. Bikur Cholim of East N.Y. (Anshe Shepetovka), 201
Cong. Bnai Isaac Anshei Lechowitz, 129
Cong. Bnai Pischei Tshuvo Anshei Aniksty, 4

Cong. Bnei Jacob Anshei Brzezan, 9
Cong. Dorshei Tov Anshei Pinsk, 165
Cong. Ezras Achim Bnei Pinsk, 165
Cong. Rabeinu Nochum Anshei Grodno, 67
Cong. Rodef Sholem Indep. Podhajcer K.U.V., 168
Cong. Tiferes Beth Jacob, Ezras Israel Anshei Bronx, 297
Cong. Tifereth Joseph Anshei Przemysl, 178
Coordinating Committee of Jewish Lands. Fed's., 170
Covadlo, Walter J., 298
Czenstochauer B.V. & U.V., 46
Czenstochauer Y.M., Inc., 46
Czenstochover Club, 46
CZERNOWITZ, 42
CZESTOCHOWA, 46
DABIE, 47
David Kantrowitz Family B.A., 265
DEBICA, 48
Deborah Rebekah Lodge No. 13, I.O.O.F., 266
Delatizer Aid B.S., 49
DELATYCZE, 49
DEMBICA, 48
Dembitzer Landsleit, Inc., 48
DIMER, 50
DINEWITZ, 51
DINOVITS, 51
DISNA, 52
Doctor Braunstein Society, 200
DOMBE, 47
Dombier B.S., 47
Dora Lipkowitz Voluntary Aid & S.B.S., 267
Drisser Bros. B.S., 19
DROGOBYCH, 53
DROHOBYCZ, 53
Duboier Young Ladies Club, 54
Duboier Y.M.P.A., Inc., 54
DUBOY, 54
DUKLA, 55
Duklar Relief Society, Inc., 55
DYATLOVO, 56
DZHURIN, 57
DZISNA, 52
Dzuriker S.B.A., 125
East Bronx Cultural Society, 12
Elinitzer K.U.V., 73

ELIZABETHGRAD, 83
Empire State Lodge No. 460, I.O.O.F. 268
Epstein U.V., 152
Ershte Bolshowcer S.B.S. & Lodge No. 517, I.O.B.A., 20
Erste Budzanower K.U.V., 34
Erste Jaworower K.U.V., 244
Erste Kopyczyncer K.U.V., 94
Erste Sadagorer K.U.V., 195
Erste Sandowa Wishner K.U.V., 299
Erste Tauster U.V., 228
Erste Trembowler K.U.V., 226
Erster Bacauer Rom. K.U.V., 5
Erster Knihinin Stanislauer K.U.V., 86
Erster Krzywcza An San B.S., 107
Erster Samborer K.U.V., 196, 197
Family Lodge No. 189, I.O.B.A., 269
FASTOV, 58
Federation of Bessarabian Societies, Inc., 14
Federation of Bess. Societies of America, 11
Federation of Polish Jews in America, 170
First Austiler Aid Society, 234
First Bacauer Rumanian American K.U.V., 5
First Bacauer S.B.A, 5
First Beitcher S.B.S., 15
First Belzer Bess. S.B.A., 8
First Bratslow Podolier S.B.S., 24
First Bratslower Ladies Aux., 25
First Britchaner B.A., Inc., 27
First Dimerer Prog. Society, 50
First Djouriner Podolier Alliance, Inc., 57
First Horodenker S.B.S., 63
First Indep. Loposhner Society, Inc., 125
First Indep. Mikulincer S.B.A., 138
First Indep. Odesser Ladies S.B.A., 156
First Indep. Storoznetzer Buk. S.B.A., 217
First Indep. Zinkower Society, 258
First Klevaner S.B.S., 84
First Klimontover S.B.S., 85
First Kopyczynzer S.B.S., 94

First Koropiecer B.A., 96
First Krasner S.B.S., 186
First Krasnobroder Aid Society, 103
First Krasnystauer Y.M.B.S., 104
First Krystonopoler S.B.S., 111
First Kulaczkowitzer K.U.V., 113
First Ladies Krementshuger B.A., 105
First Lesznower S.B.S. Sons of Jacob Solomon, 117
First Luberer B.A., 130
First Lutzker B.A., 128
First Mikulinzer Lodge No. 556, I.O.B.A., 138
First Ottynier Y.M.B.A., 162
First Pogrebisht B.S., Inc., 169
First Povolotcher S.B.A., 172
First Prager Indep. Assn., Inc., 174
First Pressburger S.B.S., 23
First Probuzna S.B.S., 176
First Prog. Ladies of Dinewitz, 51
First Proskurover Y.M.P.A.. 177
First Przemysler S.B.S., 179
First Radomer Cong., Chebra Agudas Achim Anshei Radom, 181
First Rashkower B.S., Inc., 187
First Rozishtcher B.A., 193
First Samborer K.U.V., 196, 197
First Sokoroner Dr. Braunstein Prog. Society, 200
First Soroker Bess. Ladies Aid Society, 210
First Soroker Bess. Mutual Aid Society, 210
First Stryjer Sisters B.S., 218
First Tlumatcher B.S., 302
First Uscie Zielone S.B.A., 233
First Ushitzer Podoler B.A., Inc., 212
First Washkoutz Bucowinaer S.B.S., 235
First Wiznitz Buk. Ladies Society, Inc., 237
First Wojnilower Lodge No. 674, I.O.B.A., 238
First Wojnilower S.B.S., 238
First Yezierna S.B.S., 75
First Zawichoster Y.M.B.A., 248
First Zbarazer Relief Society, 249
First Zborower S.B.A., 250

First Zdunska Wola B.S., 251
First Zelechover Prog. Society, 252
First Zinkowitzer Pod. K.U.V., 260
Free Sons of Judah, see Indep. Order Free Sons of Judah
Friends of Alexandrovsk B.A., Inc., 1
Friends of Grodno, 67
GABIN, 59
GALICIA, 60, 61
Gatherers of the Sound of Love of Life, 273
GERMANY, 62
Goldfaden Camp No. 9, Order Bnai Zion, 270
Goldstein, Taube B.S., 198
GOMBIN, 59
Gombiner Y.M.B.A., Inc., 59
GORODENKA, 63
GORODISHCHE, 64
Grodner Club, 67
Grodner-Lipkaner Br. 74, W.C., 65
Grodner Patronat, 67
Grodner Relief Alliance of the U.S. & Canada, 67
GRODNO, 65, 66, 67
Grodno of Philadelphia Lodge No. 259, I.O.B.A., 67
GRODZISK (MAZOWIECKI), 68
Grodzisker Mutual Aid Society, 68
Guskin, Reuben, Babroisker Br. 206, W.C., 18
GUSYATIN, 69
Hatikvo B.S., Inc., 271
Heit, Ray, Chapter of the Kittever Ladies Relief Aux., 116
Henry Clay Lodge No. 15, I.O.B.A., 166
Hersh Rabinovitch, 159
Hilfs Committee for the Smela Political Convicts, 41
Hirsch Liska Lodge No. 66, O.B.A., 278
HORODENKA, 63
Horodishter Korsoner Lodge, Inc., 64
HORODYSZCZE, 64
HOTIN, 81
HUNGARY, 70, 71, 72
HUSIATYN, 69
Husiatyner-Podolier Friendship Circle, 69
IGUMEN, 43

Igumener Indep. B.A., 43
ILINTSY, 73
Indep. Berlader B.A., 6
Indep. Brodsky B.A., Inc., 272
Indep. Bukarester Sick Aid Ass'n., 33
Indep. Burdujener S.B.S., 35
Indep. Elizabethgrad Ladies B.A., 83
Indep. Fremtsche Radimnauer Frauen K.U.V., 184
Indep. Frymcie Radymnoer Frauen K.U.V., 184
Indep. Greater New York S.B.A., 147
Indep. Grodno S.S.S., 67
Indep. Jaworower Ass'n., 244
Indep. Kinsker Aid Ass'n., 91
Indep. Lutzker Aid Society, 128
Indep. Lutzker Aid Society, Ladies Aux., 128
Indep. Meseritzer Y.M.A., 134
Indep. Mogelnitzer B.S., 140
Indep. Nemirover B.S., Inc., 145
Indep. Opoler B.S., 157
Indep. Opoler Ladies Aux., 157
Indep. Order Brith Abraham (see also Order Brith Abraham), 20, 67, 87, 138, 160, 166, 207, 238, 269, 272, 290, 295
Indep. Order Free Sons of Judah, 253
Indep. Order of Odd Fellows, 72, 266, 268, 277
Indep. Orler B.S., Inc., 158
Indep. Proskurover Society, 177
Indep. Rohatyner Y.M.B.A., 191
Indep. Skierniewicer B.A., 205
Indep. Tarnower K.U.V., 223
Indep. Zetler Y.M.B.A., 56
International Workers' Order, 12, 46
Israelite Fraternity of Brooklyn, Inc., 30
JAKOBSTADT, 110
JANOW, 74
JAWOROW, 244
JEKABPILS, 110
JEZIERNA, 75
Joint Smela Relief, Inc., 41
Joseph Kessler, 28
Joseph, Moses, United Family of, 292

Kalisher Ladies Society, Inc., 77
Kalisher Lands. & Vicinity, W.C. Br. 361, 300
Kalisher Non Partisan Relief Committee, 300
Kalisher Social Verein, 76
KALISZ, 76
KALUSH, 77
Kalusher Ladies Society, Inc., 77
KALUSZ, 77
Kaluszer Ladies Society, Inc., 77
KAMENETS, 78
KAMENETS-PODOLSKI, 79, 260
Kamenetz-Litovsker U.V., 78
Kamenetz-Podoler Relief Org., 79
Kamenetz-Litovsker Women's Malbish Arumim League, 78
Kamenetzer Litovsker Memorial Committee, 78
Kamenetzer Podolier B.A., 260
KAMIENIEC LITEWSKI, 78
Kantrowitz, David, Family B.A., 265
KEDAINIAI, 80
Keidaner Ass'n., 80
Keidaner Ladies Aid Society, 80
KEIDANY, 80
Kessler, Joseph, 28
Khevre Kedishe Anshey Shklover, 202
Khevre Kol Ahavas Khayim, 273
Khevre Lomza V'Gatch, 124
KHOTIN, 81
KIELCE, 82
Kieltzer & Chenchiner Relief Committee, 82
Kieltzer S.B.S. of New York, 82
KINSK, 91
Kipiler Y.M.B.A., 95
KIROVOGRAD, 83
Kittever Ladies Relief Aux., 116
Kletzker B.U.F., 297
KLEVAN, KLEWAN, 84
KLIMONTOW, 85
Klub Zyrardow, 262
KNIHININ, 86
Kodima B.S., Inc., 274
Kolbushover Teitelbaum Wallach Lodge No. 98, I.O.B.A., 87
KOLBUSZOWA, 87, 88
Kolbuszowa Relief Ass'n., Inc., 87
Kolbuszower Teitelbaum Ferbriderungs Ferayn Cong., 87

Kolbuszower Y.M.B.S., 88
KOLO, 89
Kolomear Friends Ass'n., 90
KOLOMYYA, 90
KONSK, KONSKIE, 91
Kopister B.A., 92
KOPISTY, 92
KOPRZYWNICA, 93
KOPYCHINTSY, 94
KOPYCZYNCE, 94
KOPYL, 95
KOROPETS, 96
KOROPIEC, 96
Korostishever Aid Society, 97
KOROSTYSHEV, 97
KORSUN, 64, 98
KOSICE, 99
Kosice & Vicinity Ch. 59, Bnai Zion, 99
Kossuth Ass'n. of New York, Inc., 71
KOVEL, 100
KRAKES, 101
KRASNIK, 102
KRASNOBROD, 103
KRASNY GORODOK, 186
KRASNYSTAW, 104
Kreitzburger-Jacobstadter B.A., 110
KREMENCHUG, 105
KREMENETS, 106
Kremenitzer Wolyner B.A., 106
Krementchuger Ladies B.A., Inc., 105
KREUZBERG, 110
KRIVICHI, 107, 108
KIRVOYE OZERO, 109
Krivozer Fraternal Society of Greater New York, 109
KROK, 101
Kroker B.A., 101
KRUSTPILS, 110
KRYSTYNOPOL, 111
KRZEMIENIEC, 106
KRZYWICZE, 107, 108
KUDRYNCE, 112
Kudryncer B.S., Inc., 112
KULACZKOWCE, 113
Kupersmith, Monish, Kupiner Circle, 114
KUPIN, 114
Kupiner Podolier Br. 329, W.C., 114

Kupiner-Podolier Memorial Committee, 114
KUTNO, 115
Kutno Society Bnai Jacob, 115
KUTY, 116
LACHOWICZE, 129
Lady McKinley B.S., 275
Lady McKinley Lodge, 275
Lahishin S.B.S., 122
Lahishiner Ladies Aux., 122
LAHISZYN, 122
Landsmanshaftn, Subject Collection, 303
Latichever Prog. Soc., Inc., 118
Leah B.S., 276
Lechowitzer Ladies Aux., 129
LESZNIOW, 117
LETICHEV, 118
LIPKANY, see also 65
Lipkowitz, Dora, Voluntary Aid & S.B.S., 267
Liska, Hirsch, Lodge No. 66, O.B.A., 278
LODZ, 119, 120, 121
Lodzer Young Ladies Aid Soc., 119
Lodzer Y.M.B.S., 120
LOGISHIN, 122
Lomazer Y.M. & W.B.A., Inc., 123
LOMAZY, 10, 123
LOMZA, 124
Lomzer Aid Society, 124
Lomzer Ladies Relief Society, 124
Lopates Family Circle, 78
LOPUSZNA, 125
Loyal American Lodge No. 402, I.O.O.F., 277
Loyal B.S., Inc., 278
LUBAN, 126
Lubaner & Vicinity B.S., 126
LUBER, 130
LUCK, 128
LUTOWISKA, 127
Lutowisker Y.M.B.S., 127
LUTSK, 128
Lutzker Br. 538, W.C., 128
LYAKHOVICHI, 129
LYUBAR, 130
Makover U.V., 131
MAKOW (MAZOWIECKI), 131, 132
Makower Y.M.A.S., 132
Marcus, Nathan, B.S., Inc., 283

Max Rosh B.S. of Harlem, Inc., 279
McKinley, Lady, B.S. (Lodge), 275
Mendelsohn, Moses, Lodge No. 91, I.O.B.A., 295
Menorah B.S., Inc., 280
MESERITS, 134, 135
Michalpolier Podolier B.A., 136
MIDDLE VILLAGE, 133
Middle Village B.A., Inc., 133
MIEDZYRZEC (PODLASKI), 134, 135
MIKHAILOVKA, 136
MIKHALPOL, 136
MIKULINCE, 137, 138
Mikulincer Indep. Lodge, Inc., 137
MIKULINTSY, 137, 138
MINSK, 139
Minsker Ladies B.S., 139
MISHNITS, 142
MOGELNITSE, 140
MOGIELNICA, 140
MOGILEV, 141
MOHILEV, 141
Monish Kupersmith Kupiner Circle, 114
Mordecai Lodge No. 29, O.B.A., 271
Moses Family Society, Inc., 281
Moses Joseph, United Family of, 292
Moses Mendelsohn Lodge No. 91, I.O.B.A., 295
Mount Sinai Hebrew Mutual B.S., 282
MYSZYNIEC, 142
Narevker Ladies Aux., 143
Narevker U.V., 143
NAREW, 143
NASHELSK, 144
Nashelsker Br. 622, W.C., 173
Nashelsker Society of Los Angeles, 144
NASIELSK, 144
Nathan Marcus B.S., Inc., 283
National Council for Bessarabian Jews, 13
National Jewish Ukrainian Committee of the Jewish Council for Russian War Relief, 231
NAYSHTUT, 152
NEMENZIN, 148
Nemenziner B.A., 148
NEMIROV, 145
NEUSTADT, 152
Neustadter Prog. Y.M.B.A., 152
New Nook Ass'n., 177
NEW YORK, 146, 147
New York Social Club, 146
Nickolayever U.V. of Chicago, 149
NIEMENCZYN, 148
NIKOLAYEV, 149
Nocomo Club, Inc., 284
NOVOSELITSA, 150
NOVYE STRELISHCHE, 151
NOWY KORCZYN, 152
NOWY SACZ, 153
ODESSA, 154, 155, 156
Odessa Y.M. of Harlem S.B.A., 154
Odessar Y.M.B.A., 155
Onward Society, 301
OPOLE, 157
Order Bnai Zion, 270
Order Brith Abraham, 271, 278
ORLA, 158
OSTRE, 159
OSTROG, 159
OSTROLEKA, 160, 161
OSTROLENKA, 160, 161
Ostrolenker Friendship Society, Inc., 160
Ostrolenker Lodge No. 607, I.O.B.A., 160
Ostrolenker Prog. Y.F., 161
OTTYNIA, 162
OTYNYA, 162
OZAROW, 163
Ozarower Y.M.S., 163
Pannonia Lodge No. 185, I.O.O.F., 72
Pannonia Rebekah Lodge No 130, I.O.O.F., 72
Paul Revere Lodge No. 464, B.A. 207
Philip Bernstein S.B.A., Inc., 285
PIATEGORSK, 164
PIATIGORY, 164
Piaterer Prog. B.S., Inc., 164
Piliver Podolier Society, Inc., 180
PINSK, 165
PLOCK, 166, 167
PLOTSK, 166, 167
Plotzker Y.M.I.A., 167
PODGAITSY, 168
PODHAJCE, 168

Podolier Br. 277, I.W.O., 12
POGREBISHCHE, 169
POGREBISHCHENSK, 169
POKSHIVNITSA, 93
Pokshivnitzer Relief Committee, 93
POLAND, 170
POLOTSK, 171
Polotzker Workingmen's B.S., 171
POVOLOCH, 172
PRAGA WARSZAWSKA, 173, 174
Prager-Warschauer Br. 386, W.C., 173
PRESSBURG, 23
PRILUKI, 175
PROBEZHNA, 176
PROBUZNA, 176
Progress Mutual Aid Society, 286
Prog. Horodenker B.S., Inc., 63
Prog. Kovler Y.F. Br. 475, W.C., 100
Prog. Mishnitzer Y.M.S., 142
Prog. Samborer Y.M.B.A., 197
PROSKUROV, 177
Proskurover Ladies B.A., 177
Prudential B.A., Inc., 175
PRZEMYSL, 178, 179
Przemysler Central Relief Society, Inc., 179
PYLYAVA, 180
Rabinovitch, Hersh, 159
RADOM, 181, 182
RADOMYSHL, RADOMYSYL, 183
Radomysler B.S., 183
Radomysler Ladies Aux. of Chicago, 183
RADYMNO, 184
Radziner Prog. Society, Inc., 185
Radziviller-Woliner B.A., 44
RADZIVILOV, 44
RADZIWILLOW, 44
RADZYN (PODLASKI), 185
RAIGORODOK, 186
Rappaport Family Circle, Inc., 287
RASCHKOW, 187
RASZKOW, 187
RATCHEV, 189
Ratchever-Volyner Aid Ass'n., Inc., 189
RAYGORODOK, 186
Ray Heit Chapter of the Kittever Ladies Relief Aux., 116

Rebekah Assembly, I.O.O.F., 72, 266
Reuben Guskin Babroisker Br. 206, W.C., 18
Revere, Paul, Lodge No. 464, B.A., 207
REZEKNE, 188
REZHITSA, 188
Riazanifker B.A., Inc., 194
ROGACHEV, 189
ROGATIN, 190, 191
ROHATYN, 190, 191
Rohatyner Y.M.S., Inc., 190
Rose Schwartz, 14
Rosh, Max, B.S. of Harlem, Inc., 279
ROZAN, 192
Rozaner Ladies B.A., Inc., 192
ROZHAN, 192
ROZHISHCHE, 193
ROZYSZCZE, 193
RYZHANOVKA, 194
SADAGURA, 195
SADGORA, 195
Samaritan Society, 60
SAMBOR, 196, 197
SADOWA WISZNIA, 299
Sandzer Society, Inc., 153
SANZ, 153
SATANOV, 198, 199
Satanover B.S., 198
Satanover Relief Committee, 198
Satanover Sisterhood, 199
Schatz, Boris, B.S., Inc., 166
Schklover Indep. B.A., Inc., 202
Schoenberg Family Aid Society, 289
Schwartz, Rose, 14
SECURENI, 200
SEKIRYANY, 200
Selective Bros. of Israel, Inc., 288
Shedlowtzer B.A., 222
SHEPETOVKA, 201
SHIDLOVETS, 222
SHKLOV, 202
Shonberg Family Aid Society, 289
SHUMSK, 10
Sisterhood of Grodno, 67
SKALA, 203
Skalar B.S., 203
SKIDEL, 204
Skidler B.A., 204
SKIERNIEWICE, 205

SMELA, see also 41
Smiller B.A. of Philadelphia, 41
SMOLEVICHI, 206
SNIATYN, 207
Sniatyner American Lodge, Inc., 207
SNYATYN, 207
SOKORONE, 200
Soler Bros. B.A., 208
SOLY, 208
SOPOCKINE, see also 66
SOPOTSKIN, see also 66
SOROCA, 10, 209, 210
Soroker Y.F.B. & E. League, 209
SOROKI, 10, 209, 210
Stabiner Y.M.B.A., 221
Stanislauer Prog. B.A., 211
STANISLAV, 211
STARAYA USHITSA, 212
Stavisker Y.M.B.A., 213
STAVISKI, STAWISKI, 213
STOLIN, 214
Stoliner Prog. Society, Inc., 214
STOPNICA, 215, 216
STOPNITS, 215, 216
Stopnitzer Y.M.B.A., 215
STOROZHINETS, 217
Strelisker Y.M.B.A., 151
STRY, STRYJ, 218
STRZELISKA, NOWE, 151
Subject Collection Landsmanshaftn, 303
SVISLOCH, 219
SWISLOCZ, 219
Swislotcher B.A., 219
SZCZENIEC, 220
Szenicer Ladies S.B.S., 220
SZTABIN, 221
SZYDLOWIEC, 222
TARNOW, 223
Taube Goldstein B.S., 198
Tchausser Society, 39
TEREBOVLYA, 224, 225, 226
TIMKOVICHI, 227
TLUMACZ, 302
Tolchiner B.S., 229
TOUSTE, 228
TREMBOWLA, 224, 225, 226
Trembowla True Sisters, Inc., 224
Tremont B.S., Inc., 290
Trisker Voliner Y.M.B.A., 230
True Brethren B.A., 291
Tsvishn Kolomear Y.F., 90

TULCHIN, 229
TURISK, 230
TURZYSK, 230
UKRAINE, 231
ULLA, 232
Uller B.A., 232
United Antepoler Ass'n., 3
United Austiler Relief Committee, 234
United Bessarabian Federation, 11
United Botoshaner American Brotherly & B.A., 21
United Brisker Relief, 26
United Bros. Town of Smila, 41
United Chmielniker Relief Committee, 45
United Czestochowa Relief Committee, 46
United Disner B.A., 52
United Emergency Relief Committee for the City of Lodz, 121
United Family of Moses Joseph, 292
United Fastoffer No. 1, Inc., 58
United Friends of Czernowitz, 42
United Grodner Relief, 67
United Horodenker Relief Committee, 63
United Jewish Organizations, 293
United Lodzer Relief Committee, 121
United Lomzer Relief Committee, 124
United Lutzker Relief Committee, 128
United Lutzker Y.M. & Y.L. Ass'n., 128
United Meseritzer Relief, Inc., 135
United Nashelsker Relief Society of Los Angeles, 144
United Neustadter-Epstein Society of New York, 152
United Novoselitzer Relief, Inc., 150
United Proskurover Relief, 177
United Radomer Relief for U.S. & Canada, Inc., 182
United Relief for Przemysl, 178
United Rozaner Relief Committee of New York, 192

United Samborer Ladies Relief Society, 197
United Samborer Orphans Org., 197
United Samborer Relief Society, 197
United Smolewitzer Ass'n., Inc., 206
United Sons of Israel, Inc., 294
United Sons of Israel, Ladies Aux., 294
United Sons of Israel of the Bronx, Inc., 294
United Zaromber Relief Committee, 247
Unity Friendship League, Inc., and/or Moses Mendelsohn Lodge No. 91, I.O.B.A., 295
USCIE ZIELONE, 233
USCILUG, 234
USHITSE PODOLYE, 212
USTILUG, 234
VASCKAUTI, 235
VASHKOVTSY, 235
VILEIKA, VILEYKA, 236
Vileika Aid Ass'n. of Lynn, Mass., 236
VIZHNITSA, 237
VOINILOV, 238
VOLKOVYSK, 239, 240
VOYNILOV, 238
Walter J. Covadlo, 298
WARSAW, 173, 174, 241, 242
Warschauer B.S., Inc., 241
WASHKOUTZ, 235
Weiss, Chaim Hersch, First Janover S.B.A., 74
WIZNITZ, 237
WLOCLAWEK, 243
Wloclawker Chebra Ahabath Achim, 243
WOJNILOW, 238
WOLKOWYSK, 239, 240
Wolkowysker Relief Society, 239
Workmen's Circle, 18, 61, 65, 100, 114, 128, 173, 257, 262
Workmen's Circle Br. 42, 61
World Federation of Bessarabian Jews, 13
YAVOROV, 244
YEKABPILS, 110
YELIZAVETGRAD, 83
YEZIERNE, 75
Young Krevitzer, 108
ZABLUDOW, 245
Zabludower Yisker Book Committee, 245
ZALESHCHIKI, 246
Zaleszczyker K.U.V., 246
ZALESZCZYKI, 246
ZAREBY KOSCIELNE, 247
ZAREMBY, 247
Zaromber Israel Aid Society, 247
Zashkover K.U.V. of New York, 255
ZAWICHOST, 248
ZBARAZ, ZBARAZH, 249
ZBOROV, ZBOROW, 250
Zdinskawolle Lodge No. 131, Indep. Order Free Sons of Judah, 253
ZDUNSKA WOLA, 251, 253
ZDZIECIOL, 56
ZELECHOW, 252
ZETL, 56
ZGIERZ, 253
Zgierzer S.B.S., 253
ZGURITSA, 254
Zguritzer-Bess. Society, 254
ZHASHKOV, 255
ZHVANCHICK, 256
ZHVANETS, 257
ZINKOW, 258, 259
Zinkower-Podolier B.A., 259
ZINKOWITZ, 260
Zinkowitzer & Kamenetz Podolier Society, Inc., 260
ZUROW, 261
ZWANCHIK, 256
Zwanitz Podolier Prog. Br. 277, W.C., 257
Zwanitz Podolier Relief Committee, 257
Zwantchyker Podolier Y.M.B.A., Inc., 256
ZYRARDOW, 262
Zyrardow Br. 301, W.C., 262